The Cain & Abel Story

The Cain & Abel Story

An Interpretation

by
Robert Tippett

Copyright © 2014

All rights reserved. Produced in the United States of America. No part of this publication may be reproduced, or transmitted, in any form or by any means electronic, mechanical, photocopying, recording, or otherwise, without the prior written permission of the author.

ISBN 978-0-9801166-7-0
Published by Katrina Pearls, LLC

Table of Contents

Preface
      A need to know Cain and Abel 7

Introduction
      My method 13

Chapter 1
      The births of Cain and Abel 19

Chapter 2
      The purpose of Cain and Abel 35

Chapter 3
      The sin of Cain 49

Chapter 4
      The initial punishment of Cain 57

Chapter 5
      The lineage of Cain 73

Chapter 6
      The eternal punishment of Cain 101

Chapter 7
  The reincarnation of Abel 109

Conclusion
  The moral of the story. 115

Preface

A need to know Cain and Abel

I imagine there are not many adults in the Western world that do not know of Cain and Abel. The story of Cain and Abel is found only in chapter 4 of the Book of Genesis. It follows the story of Adam and Eve's fall from grace, and precedes the list of Adam's lineage, from Seth to Noah. In this one chapter, both Cain and Abel become lost sons, the ones that do not count. One kills the other, preventing him from reaching his potential. Then the killer is banished, never to have any light of history shone on him again.

As a child, in a Christian family environment, I was taught the story of Cain and Abel, but only up to the point of Cain being sent away from where he had lived. I first realized there was a lineage that Cain produced, when I began reading the Old Testament as an assignment for a church course in which I had enrolled. I was an adult who was beyond the prime of life when I first read that extended view of Cain's legacy.

The Cain & Abel Story

I cannot say that the course I was taking explained the story of Cain and Able to any degree of depth. I have no vivid memories of enlightenment that come back to me now. The lineage of Cain reads as any other chapter that also lists a string of Biblical names. Other than names being rattled off, the names have little meaning to the untrained eye. The verses telling of the lineage of Cain seem to drone on and on, about forgettable people. The mind gets bored when it has to deal with too many people begetting in a row, with no story making that begetting memorable.

The general consensus, it is safe to say, is that Cain was bad, and he was punished for his crime of murder. In searches of Cain's lineage on the Internet, there seems to be some thought that the last generation of Cain's lineage showed some potential for a positive trend, as a possible hint of redemption. This is because we find people who are identified as innovators and initiators, in such areas as music and art, developing harps and horns, while perfecting brass and bronze metalworking.

One of these has the most memorable name of Tubal-cain. There are some who debate if the name should be presented as Tubal-Cain, Tubalcain, or Tubal-cain. Several scholars see this as a tribute to Cain, the patriarch of that dead branch of Adam. The name was given to Tubal-cain by his father, Lamech. Lamech is also the name of the father of Noah, but they are two entirely different people. However promising Genesis 4 seems to be going, with the birth of children who are firsts in their crafts, we lose all sense of redemption once we find Lamech saying he has done worse than his great, great, great grandfather Cain. Lamech, it seems, had "killed a man and wounded a child," so he will be punished more for his sins than was Cain.

Recent news of the movie Noah reveals that the villain in that story is none other than Tubal-cain. The review I read told how

Preface: A need to know Cain and Abel

Tubal-cain is projected as an evil person, one who tries to influence the sons and daughters-in-law of Noah to go against their father. I find that interesting, as that could perhaps be the first scrutiny ever put on a descendant of Cain. Other than it seems probable to me that Tubal-cain and Noah did not live in the same neck of the ancient woods, at the time of the Great Flood, they probably did live at the same time.

I get a feel from Genesis that the Patriarchs remained in close proximity with one another, rather than wanting to roam a dangerous world. It seems logical for them to be less transient back then, and not like our society has evolved today. Since Cain was forced to move east of Eden, it may be that Tubal-cain felt more comfortable travelling to strange places. However, I do not see Noah and Tubal-cain having come into direct conflict with one another; but the director's view of Tubal-cain projects his character accurately ... as a villain.

I see the key to deeper understanding of Biblical scripture comes from slow and meditative reading, while acknowledging that everything comes from the Divine, to the reader, through the authors. Everything written that is in any book of the Holy Bible has deeper meaning that can immediately be realized. In addition to that method of contemplative study, one must realize that all names become a source of that meaning, because names are words that define the essence of a child, a meaning given by the father.

I had been led to that understanding in other studies of old texts, so when I began delving into the books of the Holy Bible, I would take the time to look up those in the weekly lectionary readings. In my Bible study course, we did more speed reading, where large portions of books were read each week, and so many names would roll by the eyes I had to pick and choose which

The Cain & Abel Story

ones I felt the most need to research. I was intrigued with what Genesis 4 had to offer when I first read it years ago, but I did not look deeper into the name meanings then.

I could sense that more was there under the surface that was important to know. I had been intrigued by the concept of the "mark of Cain" and wanted to see if I could get a better handle on what that meant. Because I always had something that I deemed to be more important work, things like pondering the meaning of one short chapter in Genesis was quickly filed into the "to do" folder. As time rolled on, other interests were sorted on top of that. As much as I wanted to delve into Cain and Abel, it sat and patiently waited for me to come back to it.

Over the past month or more, I have finally taken the time to approach the verses that tell the story of Cain and Abel. As is always the case when Scripture is contemplated, I was amazed at what poured forth from the words written. I find that it is a most important story to understand properly because it represents a first theme, one which is repeated throughout the stories held in the Holy Bible. When one understands the meaning of the Cain and Abel story, one has been given a template that not only fits the history of the Old Testament, it fits the present day and beyond.

The story of Cain and Abel is more than a story of "two brothers." It is the story of each of us. We continuously struggle with influences that ask us to do good and ask us to do evil. This makes it vital to know the full truth of what is written in the Cain and Abel story. It mirrors just how beautifully the Holy Bible can only be the construction of the mind of God, with the main characters being those of the living vine who produced good fruit. All those who fall to the wayside become dead branches, or unkempt vines that produce wild grapes. All that begins with

Preface: A need to know Cain and Abel

the story told in Genesis 4, of Cain and Abel.

I warn you, I have some views that may shake your preconceptions of the foundations of Christianity. The history lesson that comes from the Book of Genesis is intended to show a world teeming with sin, but a world that did not know the meaning of sin. Everything that you consider to be the darkest places of modern day life; horrendous things that commonly occur and seem too frightening to even peek at, they all existed at the time of Adam and Eve. That black image of the world is brought out in the story of Cain and Abel.

I present this work as a testament of my faith. I was led to write what is exposed in this short book, as it is a topic that needs to be explained. I stand by my thoughts and visions, and I present them as a tool to strengthen your faith.

All that I have written is not all that can be seen. I welcome you to read these words and meditate on them, placing your soul in the hands of God and letting His meaning be your understanding. We have no mind of our own, if all we can think is what someone else tells us to know. You may find that I left some things out; but, that omission can be your discovery, one which will represent your own connection with the Lord, and one you will always remember.

Robert Tippett
March 27, 2014

The Cain & Abel Story

Introduction

My method

Before I begin to dissect Genesis 4 into pieces and analyse them, let me set up what you will find. There is a method to the madness.

First, I have divided the 26 verses into parts that correspond to shifts in the storyline. As such, the birth of Cain and Abel is in itself a separate part, followed by the separate part that places focus on the time when they made offerings to the Lord. This is followed by the jealousy that overtook Cain, then the punishment for his sin. His lineage arose from that banishment, and one that is presented, the reader is returned to focus on Adam and Eve having another child. In all, you will find I have divided the story of Genesis 4 into six parts. Each part is important to recognize as a purposeful step towards complete understanding of the whole.

The Cain & Abel Story

Second, each verse is introduced in three ways. The first way is a standard translation, which is primarily the King James Version. It represents a translation that is in no way one I made up. As I have searched for an online translation that has the accompanying Hebrew, my source for most of the translations in this work is the website Bible Hub. They default to the King James version, but I may present other translations in my interpretations. Multiple English translations are found in the many different versions that are available, due to the fact that fixed words in Hebrew have variable translations.

The second way I present a verse is in the Hebrew text. This is in Hebrew letters, and is not a transliteration. I do use transliterations in the interpretation, but I present the Hebrew letters to give the effect of how strange what was written is to someone not literate in Hebrew. Again, I did not copy the Hebrew text from ancient scrolls, in order to present them here. All of the Hebrew text presented has been copied from the website Mechon Mamre, which also provides the Hebrew text with an English translation.

The Hebrew text on that website is shown as normal Hebrew text, to be read from right to left. In the copying and pasting process, the placing of the Hebrew into my document changed that presentation. Therefore, the letters of Hebrew words are ordered as English is read, from left to right.

I am not fluent in Hebrew, so I do not know all the particles and added letters that change a root word into a self-contained statement. An example could be a root verb meaning "to run," whatever that is in Hebrew. That base word could have additions to the root that could allow someone fluent in Hebrew to read that verb as, "they then ran." The word is still a statement relative to the act of running.

Introduction: My method

I do not know Hebrew, do not profess to know Hebrew, nor do I understand any of the nuances of the language. I do know how to look up a website that has a Hebrew parallel text, which shows what was written and then provides the meaning of the root word. From this I present a literal translation as the third way a verse can be read.

My rudimentary translations are, by design, not to be read as a fluid statement. They are designed to show how much has been added to what was written, so it is understandable to minds that are not fluent in the Hebrew language. Even the addition of some Hebrew marks, which guide the pronunciations and intended root meanings, were not part of the original text. I have found that the problem with translations and additions is they become paraphrases of what the author wrote, and thus they are intentionally one-dimensional. By one-dimensional, I mean that a word in Hebrew can have more than one translation, some of which are slightly different from the others, and more meanings, depending on the vowels implied. To use one fixed translation then restricts the meaning to one narrowed focus.

I believe that a broader scope allows more to be seen, all of which adds to the intended purpose. This view allows greater clarity to come from what is written. I see this broad scope as intended, but well beyond the capability of a human brain. It is, however, a capacity readily available to the mind of God, where words are purposefully chosen to be written because of the scope of their meaning.

This can be called a form of intentional amphibology, at times, where words with double meaning are intentional because multiple meanings are to be applied. This intent comes from God, and understanding one view of God's intent can be easily obtained, while broader views require assistance from God's

The Cain & Abel Story

Holy Spirit.

One place that such amphibology is discretely in play is in the presentations of names. Names are very important to understand, as they originate from Divine intent and purpose. Names in the Holy Bible are not randomly selected by parents because they like the sound of the name. It requires those not fluent in Hebrew to investigate what a Hebrew-speaking mind automatically hears when a name is mentioned. In a name, a person is identified, as well as a statement that surrounds the person. It is important to catch hold of that statement.

Still, there often is debate about a name's meaning, with many names in the Old Testament (in particular in Genesis) rooted in a language that is a kind of "proto-Hebrew." Those who have compiled lists of the Biblical name meanings go into lengths explaining this difficulty. Part of this difficulty comes from Hebrew being a language of consonants (mostly), where the same letters can mean different things, depending on which vowel one injects into the pronunciation. You will notice that I attempt to incorporate all name meanings, rather than narrow the focus to only one. I do this so the verse may be fully understood.

Finally, you will find that for the most part I interpret each verse with a focus on the individual words and their meaning(s), in the order they are written. I attempt to have each word tell a story by itself, before it can connect to the words that surround it. Because the intent of syntax in language has trained our minds to turn a whole verse into one mouthful of meaning, this only assists our subconscious training to read speedily. This style of reading holy verses does not allow for deeper comprehension.

I have found that Scripture is carefully chosen words, such that each word deserves a moment of reflection before joining its meaning to the words before and after it. Again, in this

Introduction: My method

regard, particle attachments bring other words into the mix, as an internal statement, where the parts are read as one. For instance, many lines begin with the conjunction "And," which is followed by the true beginning of the verse (such as "And then Adam ...."). The actual word "and" was not individually written, but rather blended into a root word (in the example, "Adam"). This means one should contemplate the root word's meaning, more than the additives.

By understanding this style that I use for interpreting holy documents, be warned that I do not enter into interpretation with a preconception about what I want to find written. Instead, I begin an interpretation with a confidence that the meaning will come forward to me, as I slowly read and write down my thoughts. Sometimes I stop writing and stop thinking about this work. I walk away, so thoughts can come to me later. When ideas come to mind, I often have to do follow-up research on them, because I am not a scholar in these matters. My reference library is the Internet. I simply reflect what everyone is capable of doing.

This means that as I write I may tend to ramble, more than introduce a succinct topic and then detail all the supporting items to that topic. I have not produced one outline of what I have written, as is typical of professional writers. One might find my method somewhat confusing, as I will weave thoughts together as I go, all of which come from faith more than memory.

My words are not intended to come across as an educated lecture of what many others before me have agreed the meaning of Cain and Abel must be. I do not know what opinions others have presented on this topic. I would like to think that others have made the same conclusions I have. Still, I do not feel that I, personally, am smart enough to know which translations would

The Cain & Abel Story

be the best simple statement that would lead one to a simple conclusion. I write what comes into my mind, and I am amazed with what I find.

Some of what I write may seem to go against what has traditionally been accepted by Christians as the meaning. I find it interesting to know that the Cain and Abel story is not only told in Hebrew writings, but also in the Koran and other writings of Middle Eastern origin. Each version of the story is different. Some of the others tell of Cain and Abel having twin sisters, who were to be each other's wives. I focus only on the version that is in the Book of Genesis.

I mention this because one needs to know that civilization existed prior the times of Moses, so the Genesis story is important to several religions other than Judaism and Christianity. When Moses was divinely inspired to dictate the Book of Genesis, it became recorded as the Holy version of Biblical history. The Holy Bible is a series of books that are designed to conclude with the New Testament's focus on Jesus and his Apostles. All religions that do not honor this conclusion are then reading a half-written saga, with assumptions and conjecture about the ending. This means there has been embellishment of some of the earliest stories, because the intended meaning is unclear.

The story of Cain and Abel is better understood if one can place one's self into a time when there were absolutely no forms of religion on earth. The world was prehistoric and man was animalistic, barely above the animals and plants of which he had dominion. Adam becomes God's gift to the world, for the purpose of giving that preexisting world religion, so that it might be saved. The story of Cain and Abel plays an important role in developing that theme.

Chapter 1

The birth of Cain and Abel

1 *And the man knew Eve his wife; and she conceived and bore Cain, and said: 'I have gotten a man with the help of the LORD.'*

(All Hebrew text is presented to be read left to right, not right to left.)
א ,סדָאָהָן ,עדָיָ תאֶ-חנָהּ אשָׂתּוִ; רחַתֵּן ,דלְתֵּא תאֶ-קיַוִ, רמֵאתנֻ ,יתִינקָ שיא.
תאֶ-יהֻנוָ.

A1 *Adam had relations with Eve to conceive beget with Cain to say acquire man within YHWH.*

The significance of this first verse is twofold. First, it says that Adam and Eve had sexual relations. As a result, Eve becomes pregnant. Once she gives birth, the verse makes a statement about the miracle of childbirth, and how that miracle is to be celebrated.

The Cain & Abel Story

In regards to physical intercourse, there was no mention of a sexual relationship between Adam and Eve before they were expelled from Eden. Neither was there any mention of how old Adam and Eve were, when they were tricked into eating of the fruit from the tree of knowledge of good and evil. We do know they suddenly became aware of their nakedness, which implies they were sexually mature beings at that time.

I believe Adam and Eve were immortal and heavenly creatures, until their banishment. The "garden of Eden" was not a purely physical place, as much as it was Heaven on earth. Because of this ethereal quality, there was no need to reproduce there. Adam and Eve experienced the presence of God, so they would have experienced angels too. We know they walked with talking serpents and other animals, which Adam named, but even the animals would have had no need to reproduce. As such, when Adam and Eve were banished, so too was the serpent, who also lost however many legs it once had; so the serpent could not get around that need to crawl punishment by going to earth and laying eggs that would hatch walking serpent babies. Only on the earthly plane was reproduction necessary; and because God made man and female, His plan was for reproduction to come about.

I also believe that the concept of time does not exist in Heaven, at least as it does on the earthly plane. I assume Adam and Eve were produced within the laws of physics and biological properties, with God the Father and the Earth the mother. As such, they both were created as infants, who grew into mature bodies. God watched over them and the earthly garden provided for them as they matured. The time it took Adam and Eve to grow is unknown; but it could have been that quite some earth years passed before the aging process of the earthly plane began

Chapter 1: The birth of Cain and Abel

to more rapidly number their days.

The 930 years that Adam is said to have lived (Genesis 5:5) may be the total years since his banishment to earth. We are told he was 130 when he had Seth (Genesis 5:3), but Seth was born after Cain and Abel. When one sees 930 years as a number ten times greater than a long life span today, to divide all the age numbers by ten means Adam lived 93 human-equivalent years, and then Adam sired Seth when he was 13 human-equivalent years. Since Cain and Abel were born first, one might be able to make a leap and guess Adam was roughly 10 human-equivalent years of age when he sired Cain. That is a little young to start a family, but it still represents 100 solar years. So, Adam was "born" on earth as already strong and youthful in body, possibly capable of sexual reproduction as soon as he landed on the ground east of Eden. He was probably "born" as if he were 16 human-equivalent years, which were spent in Heaven. That would count as about 160 solar years on earth (using the 10x factor), but Genesis 5 did not add that time, because those Heavenly time is irrelevant and immaterial to earth's concept of days and years.

In Heaven, I believe Adam and Eve were naive, innocent, and pure. By the time Genesis 3 tells of the serpent tricking them to eat the forbidden fruit, they were still children, regardless of how developed their bodies were. Children have no concept of nakedness, until they are taught by parents that it is good to stay clothed. Children do notice the differences between little boys and girls, and they are inquisitive about such things, rather than embarrassed. Children begin to understand sexual urges, which leads them to discover their own genitalia. This is when a sense of embarrassment sets in, leading teens to become secretive and sensitive about their bodies. When Genesis 3 said Adam and Eve

The Cain & Abel Story

became aware of their nakedness, they had reached the equivalent of puberty. God made them clothes before sending them out of Eden, but they had taken fig leaves to hide their bodies. So, Adam and Eve were like teenaged children when their banishment from the Garden of Eden came.

Once Adam and Eve are evicted from Heaven, their most immediate need is to establish a secure environment to live in. All of the basic needs for life on earth have to be met first: food-water-air, shelter, clothing, and safety. Since God's punishment of Adam meant he would labor, "through painful toil [he would] eat food from [the ground], which would produce thorns and thistle for him." (Genesis 3:17-18) All the days of Adam's life were to bring sweat to his brow, just to stay alive. There was no urgency to make babies, with such a workload placed upon his shoulders. The first 100 years Adam and Eve were "east of Eden" can then be summed up as, "Not tonight, honey. I'm too tired."

Because chapter 4 begins with a focus on the sex act, one must see that some time passes between the exile and the time to begin a family. The change has become stabilized, which means the sex act then took on an importance. Whereas there was no need to reproduce in Heaven, there was an earthly need. Minimally, Adam would have realized it would be nice to have another male around to help him with the chores. This is a model that all farm-based, agricultural societies have realized for millennia: The more free help you have, the better the yield. Thus, intercourse was less for fun and pleasure, and more for an innate, natural inclination for procreation.

In Genesis 3:16, God told Eve that her punishment for having been deceived by the serpent would be:

> "I will make your pains in childbearing very severe; with painful labor you will give birth to

Chapter 1: The birth of Cain and Abel

children. Your desire will be for your husband,
and he will rule over you."

That statement says Eve was to bear children, but having been a child of heaven, unaware of any physical changes awaiting, within her body's design, God did not make being a woman sound like much fun. If anything, God scared Eve into being afraid of sex, due to the pains of which she had been warned. Meanwhile, as Adam worked the ground for a hundred years or so, Eve learned what it meant to be a woman, in a continually cycling state. She became as all mortal women, feeling the pains associated with being designed to conceive and deliver a child. As time passed, she would also begin to have desires for Adam to be her husband, as her bodily functions would innately cause her to wish to become pregnant.

This means procreation is another necessity of mortal existence, once one has established all the basic needs and one has reached an age of physical maturity. The punishment given by God to Eve was actually that she become a mortal woman, no longer enjoying a heavenly existence. As a woman, Eve would experience labor pains giving birth to Cain, Abel, and Seth. The process of "childbearing" includes mensuration, the physical act of penetration, delivery of a baby, and then the attachment a mother has to her children, where the pains of each child are most strongly felt by the mother.

The desire to become pregnant is why Eve would desire Adam. Adam is stated to be "your husband," which implies his fathering children and her mothering them, in all aspects of parenting. Adam is thus the man who will father the children born from Eve. The word "husbandry" is relative to "tilling the earth and raising animals," such that a "husband" is the one who must sow seeds into fertile earth, in order to reproduce in the earthly realm. In Ecclesiastes we read, "There is a time for everything, and a season for every activity under the heavens: a time to be born." (Ecclesiastes 3:1-2a) Thus, the time had come when Eve was ready to receive Adam's seed.

This innate drive to bear children is then why women seek to unite with men. In Genesis 3:17, God said to Adam, "Because you listened to your wife," (NIV) which stated his sin worthy of punishment. The word written that is translated as "wife" is "*ishshah*" ("אִשָּׁה"). The word means equally "woman" and "female," rather than a word that projects parenthood. That is a statement of companionship, stating to the male, Adam, his listening to his friend of the opposite sex. At that time, in Heaven, Adam was not yet married to Eve, in the sense of "knowing."

When Adam was sentenced to know physical aches and pains, from toiling to grow food to sustain his life, he named his wife "*Chavvah*" (*haw-wah* - חַוָּה). The name means "life" or "life giver." This name is given at the time Eve would take on the importance of delivering the first of the lineage of Adam, as neither would keep their immortality in body. Thus, when Genesis 3:20 states, "And Adam named his wife Eve because she was the mother of all living," the meaning is to predict the living line of Adam, not all humanity on earth.

This element of Genesis 3 is what makes Genesis 4 begin with a statement about sexual intercourse. That is the method for continued living in all species of animals on earth. Still, the second part of verse one shows thanks given to God for the birth of Cain. Thanks were given for more than one reason.

First, that statement by Eve, in the first verse of chapter 4, shows how important it was for Adam to sire male children. The DNA God created for Adam was to be continued through male heirs. Second, Eve was rejoicing that the pain was worthwhile.

Chapter 1: The birth of Cain and Abel

It shows her relief and happiness of having a healthy child. Together, a healthy male child being born sets up a theme throughout the Old Testament, where barrenness in a woman is seen as a failure. The failure is to not continue the living line of which Eve is the first mother. Finally, the statement, "with the help of God," says the miracle of children being formed in the womb, from their growth and development to their births and beyond, is all due to God. A human brain cannot create or duplicate that feat.

In order to fully understand the naming of Cain, it helps to realize where God had placed Adam and Eve. Once Adam and Eve became mortal human beings, they were sent to live on earth to the "east" of Eden. The word translated as "east" is "*qedem*" ("קֶדֶם"), which means "aforetime." It can also translate as "front, before, forward," or "ancient time." The light of God shines perpetually in Heaven, with no need for sleep existing. On earth, however, the light of the Sun moves, with earth changing between times of light and times of darkness. The word "east" then brings a connotation of the time before the dawn, just outside the place where the light of day never ceases.

This means Adam and Eve have been placed "before" the gates of Heaven. Genesis 3:24 ends that chapter by stating, "After he drove the man out, he placed on the east side [or "in front"] of the Garden of Eden cherubim [immortals, an order of angels] and a flaming sword flashing back and forth to guard the way to the tree of life." The entrance back into Heaven was guarded by celestial phenomena, but Adam was "before" that entrance, as a human form. As such, that placement symbolizes Adam and his family as being the keepers of that entrance.

Being sent "before" Eden, means Adam's quest was to become the light to bring the sinful to know Heaven. All mankind

The Cain & Abel Story

needed to learn they were of sin and in need of repentance in the earthly realm. That step was vital "before" re-entry into the immortal side could be possible for all God's creations. Mankind would learn of this portal to God through the living line of Adam, the Son of God. Thus, the birth of children was exciting to Eve, as all descendants of Adam would become servants of the Lord, with the help of God; and their names would indicate that role.

Adam, as stated in Genesis 3:16, had rule over Eve. Adam ruled that she have a name representative of being the mother of "all the living" or "all alive" who would descend from Adam's genes. They would be the ones who, in turn, would rule over their families, as holy priests for the One God. We know that Adam and Eve are holy because they were created on the seventh day, when God rested and blessed what He had made. God then created Adam and made him caretaker of the garden He created, to prepare him for his vocation as the earth's first caretaker of human beings.

Since Adam gave Eve her name, it can then be assumed that Adam also named his sons. The name "Cain" ("*Qayin*") comes possibly from "*qin*" ("וְקַיִן"), which means, "spear." From that root comes the possibility of "*qaneh*" ("קָנֶה"), which means, "stalk, or reed." As such, we use the word "cane" to denote a walking stick, with the word rooted in the Greek "*kanna*," meaning "reed." Such material for canes has historically been found in bamboo and reeds. This means Adam gave his son a name that meant something that comes from the earth, something that grows straight and strong, yet flexible.

When we read Eve saying, "I have gotten a man with the help of the LORD," the word "*qin*" is also a verb form, which means, "to acquire." This means the name Cain has a dual meaning,

Chapter 1: The birth of Cain and Abel

such that it represents growth from the earth (one element), amid surrounding water (another element), with a hollowness that allows air (a third element) to travel between all the elements. This name then states a baby's developmental stages, which forms (earth) in a mother's fluids (water), "acquiring" oxygen (air) through the mother's blood. Still, the child was "acquired" from everything of the couple's efforts, as a gift from God to keep alive a lineage of Adam. Cain was to be the "Reed" connecting the real to the ethereal, just as a straw can allow one to breath while under water.

Eve actually said, "*qaneh ish eth YHWH*," or "acquire man with Yahweh." The word for "man" is not the same as "adam." It denotes a male born, a son, but it also recognizes the miracle of child creation. It recognizes how all functions within a mother's body are controlled from the mind of God. The mother does not cause the fertilization of her egg, nor does her mind will the cells splitting with growth. Thus, the Lord deserves praise for all his creations.

God is the source of the genetic codes that are present within all of us, and God chooses which gametes blend to determine the sex and physical characteristics of a baby shared by mother and father. This is confirmed when Jesus said, "So they are no longer two, but one flesh. Therefore what God has joined together, let no one separate." Eve recognized the union had been brought about by the LORD. Thus, Cain was a "Stalk" connecting Heaven and Earth.

---

2 *And again she bore his brother Abel. And Abel was a keeper of sheep, but Cain was a tiller of the ground.*

The Cain & Abel Story

ב וַתֹּסֶף לָלֶדֶת, אֶת-אָחִיו אֶת-הָבֶל; וַיְהִי-הֶבֶל, רֹעֵה צֹאן, וְקַיִן, הָיָה עֹבֵד אֲדָמָה.

B1 *To add beget a brother Abel come to pass Abel pasture flock Cain come to pass serve earth.*

Verse two begins with the birth of Abel, where the Hebrew states, "To add" the birth of "a brother." Since verse one said that Adam had sexual relations with Eve, leading to Cain's birth, the absence of such a statement means "Abel" is an "addition" to the "birth" of Cain. This can indicate Abel is a twin "brother," one born after Cain. This means verse two can be read as beginning with the statement of twins being born, which is significant.

The fact that twin brothers are born makes the story of Cain and Abel parallel the story of the twins Esau and Jacob. There are parallels that can be drawn to the relationship Abraham's first son, Ishmael, had with his step-brother, Isaac. Because Joseph was the youngest (twelfth) of Jacob's sons and David was the youngest (seventh) of Jesse's sons, the aspect of the youngest born can be linked to the story of Cain and Abel. One can even see the parable told by Jesus, of the prodigal son, as having similarities involving older and younger brothers. The story of Cain and Abel is then the first story told in the Holy Bible that becomes the standard for how brothers interact with one another.

Adam chose the name Abel for his second son. That choice of name has confused many people, because the verb "*habal*" ("לָבַה") means, "act emptily" or "become vain." On the other hand, the noun "*habel*" ("לֶבֶה") means "vapor" or "breath." Experts say this meaning presents the name, "in the negative

Chapter 1: The birth of Cain and Abel

sense of having no substance and being something very close to nothing." However, this name, when combined with the name for Cain, makes perfect sense for twins.

As one egg splits to create identical twins, each son would be representative of one-half of a dual nature. Combined they represent the "reed" and the "space" within its conduit. One is the body, while the other is the soul (or breath). The dual nature of the names given to Cain ("Reed") and Abel ("Vapor") means two are one: that of earth with that of heaven. This is then representative of the duality that exists in all human beings, as we all have our physical form and bodily needs, while we all receive our life from the unseen air we breathe, with an unseen soul residing in the body.

The spiritual side of humanity is not something that animals realize. Adam and Eve had been placed into a world that was created before they were created (the sixth day versus the seventh day). They arrived in that world knowing of good and evil, of both heavenly and earthly, after eating the "fruit" that brought their enlightenment. Prior to that event, neither Adam nor Eve had any concept of anything but good.

As for the preexisting human life forms on earth, those with evolving brains, walking upright and herding animals, they did not yet know this ethereal aspect existed. They had no concept that Heaven was possible for them, much less the goal. That is the core message of religion: You are more than matter.

Because the human beings of the sixth day were without any knowledge of Heaven, they had no knowledge of sin. They were not aware of any duality. That would need to be taught to them, so that awareness of a return to heaven – a spiritual existence – was possible for them. Thus, the names of Cain and Abel, as twins from one cell, reflect this purpose as priests, missionaries,

The Cain & Abel Story

sent by God.

Cain and Abel represented the beginning of a line of priests that would be born of holy blood. Just as their parents had been formed of the earth and filled with the spirit of God's breath, God placed them on earth for the purpose of bringing religion to the world. Cain was to be a priest honoring the physical nature of mankind. Man must make the body the temple for the soul, so the land must reflect a body that must be cared for, protected, and respected. Abel, on the other hand, was to be a priest honoring the spiritual nature, listening to the voice within. Together, Heaven and Earth can be joined in a holy union.

Due to those responsibilities, Cain "was a tiller of the earth." He would "serve earth." Abel "was a keeper of sheep," which are air-breathing beings. He would "pasture flocks." Cain cultivated that which produced oxygen as a by-product of yielding foods and fruit that nurtured animal life. Abel, on the other hand, raised that which fertilized the earth, and which depended on an overseer to guide them to greener pastures.

This aspect of Cain and Abel, where their names distinguish them as individuals serving opposing natures, also denotes their service as having dual aspects that reflect the mother and the father. Cain, as a servant of the ground, is thus in close relationship with the mother principle. We are given a hint of this when Eve remarked that God had given her a son when Cain was born. No such remark was made about God producing another male offspring, when Abel was born. Therefore, Abel serves the father principle, which is shown in his overseeing a flock (either sheep or cattle).

When one is able to see the priestly intent of Adam being placed on earth, at the pathway to Heaven, we can see how Adam taught his sons to revere God the Father. We know that when

Chapter 1: The birth of Cain and Abel

both sons reached the age when they were expected to make their first sacrifices to Heaven. Both Cain and Abel take the best of their labors to be sacrificed in a religious rite to the gods. However, one is seen as pleasing to God, with the other disregarded.

This is a vital element to understand. When Abel sacrifices the fat of the yearling(s) on an altar, God looks upon this as an honor to Him. When Cain offered a sacrifice of non-breathing plants, God does not look upon this because it is not properly sacrificed to the LORD, but to the Earth goddess. This is yet another duality that matches the naming of Cain and Abel, as that visible (Reed) and that invisible (Vapor), where God the Father, who despite being invisible is known to be present, is complimented by Earth the Mother, who despite being ever visible and present is invisible as one worthy of receiving sacrifice. It is why God gave Adam dominion over Eve, but because God made a commandment to honor both mother and father, dominion does not mean a right to abuse or ignore. Both are of equal importance and require equal respect.

As difficult as it may be to some, to see polytheism written into the Genesis stories, it is plainly written in the first chapter of Genesis. The LORD God YAHWEH made His creations with the help of lesser gods. The plural form of God is present in the Hebrew word "*elohim*" ("אֱלֹהִים"), which means "gods."

The plural pronoun was used to denote "man" being created on the sixth day, in their image. God said, "Let us make mankind in our image, in our likeness." (Genesis 1:26) Likewise, when Adam and Eve were evicted from Eden, God said, "Behold, the man has become like one of Us, to know good and evil. And now, lest he put out his hand and take also of the tree of life, and eat, and live forever." (Genesis 3:22a) One of "us" could include the cherubim that were placed at the entrance to the Gar-

The Cain & Abel Story

den of Eden. So, the proof is that God used helpers, just as Santa Claus uses elves.

The creation, as stated in Genesis 1:1 says, "In the beginning God created heaven and earth" ("*shamayim eth erets*"). This means God created the gods of the heavenly realm ("*shamayim*") first, due to the order of the words written. It was then later, as an addition ("*eth*" as "and"), when God created the physical properties of the material realm ("*erets*"). One came before the other (heavens first, then earth), just as Cain came before Abel, and Adam came before Eve. Thus, after God created heavenly assistants, they assisted God in the creation of the material realm.

The purpose originates from God, regardless that God used the assistance of angels and lesser gods to make plants and animals, including man and woman, on the sixth day of the Creation. God used the Mother Earth (a goddess) to create Adam, on the seventh day, the 'day' blessed as holy by God. God's use of gods in His Creation is no different from God using human priests to teach the human flock to know God.

Our earth assisted, by becoming the mother of Adam and Eve, providing the "dust" or "clay" into which God breathed. She received the seed (DNA of God) and God breathed life into the form He molded, once it was out of the mother's womb. The same molding by God is present in all animals of earth, which is why Eve proclaimed her son was from the help of God. However, Adam was born of holy ground, as was Eve, in the place that was heaven on earth.

Because Adam and Eve were not like mere mortals, the ones born only of this earth, they were themselves "*elohim*," in the sense they were demigods. In Greek mythology, they would be called "heroes," half god and half human, possessing special powers and longevity in life. The difference is that Adam and

Chapter 1: The birth of Cain and Abel

Eve became fully human, albeit with a purity that allowed them and their bloodline to live ten times longer than mere mortals. They would not try to take advantage of their holy heritage. They would only promote belief in the One God, and ask their sons to act as priests to YAHWEH.

As we will see, being banished to earth to be a priest to God did not come with a handbook and procedures that had to be followed. One can assume that Adam's promotion of God as the one to whom sacrifices were to be made was his own error, by not promoting sacrifices to the Earth goddess as well. God would let them know more about how they should act, as they would make errors. God foresaw trial and error as yielding more lasting lessons.

The Cain & Abel Story

Chapter 2

The purpose of Cain and Abel

3 *And in process of time it came to pass, that Cain brought of the fruit of the ground an offering unto the LORD.*

ג וַיְהִי, מִקֵּץ יָמִים; וַיָּבֵא קַיִן מִפְּרִי הָאֲדָמָה, מִנְחָה--לַיהוָה.

G1 *To become goal day to come Cain fruit of earth offering YHWH.*

The beginning of this verse projects a passage of time. At the end of verse two we saw the responsibilities each child was given: Cain was a tiller of the earth; and Abel was a keeper of the flock. That statement assumes its own passage of time, enough to grow two infant boys to boys capable of fulfilling those roles. Considering the ten times rule of thumb, if Cain and Abel began working the fields with minimum supervision from Adam, say around the human-equivalent age of ten, then a hundred years

The Cain & Abel Story

had passed to reach that point in time. Adam would have taught the art of piling rocks to form an altar, and how to start a fire, before the boys would be expected to make their own sacrifices to the Lord. Thus, the passage of time that is stated in verse three is intended to show that proper preparation and training took place.

The Hebrew "*hayah*" ("יְהִי") means, "to become, to come to pass," or "to be." The word "*qets*" ("יְקֵמ") means, "end," as the "highest peak, limit, goal" or "course." The use of those words means the reader is directed to expect the passing of time to reach an objective. That objective is the "day, age, birthday, time," or the "first" ("*yom* or *ya-mim*" – "יָמִים") important milestone in the development of the children. For Cain, that "goal day" was timed by the harvesting of the fruit of the earth, the fruit of his labors.

When one understands that God knew Adam would have to leave Heaven and serve as the first priest teaching humans to believe in the One God, then one knows Adam would teach his children how to serve YAHWEH. Adam was sentenced to toil on the land, as stated in Genesis 3:17b-19a.

> "Cursed is the ground because of you; through
> painful toil you will eat food from it all the days
> of your life. It will produce thorns and thistles
> for you, and you will eat the plants of the field.
> By the sweat of your brow you will eat your
> food until you return to the ground."

This shows that Adam's first born son was raised to handle the hardest part of Adam's responsibility, which was to grow fruits and vegetables for his family's survival. Cain helped Adam grow the crops and harvest the fruits and vegetables. The spring is typically the time for planting, and the end of summer, into early fall (September-October) is when the harvest of most

Chapter 2: The purpose of Cain and Abel

crops takes place. The first fruits are typically picked earlier in the year.

The Jews celebrate this in the presentation of the First Fruits on the 16th of Nissan, at the beginning of the Festival of the Unleavened Bread (Passover). On the 6th of Divan, the Festival of Weeks takes place, called *Shavout*. This occurs in late May and early June, fifty days later. However, verse three is less about the timing during a solar year and more important as telling of the time when Cain would be responsible for making an offering to the LORD.

Cain can be seen as a newly "ordained" priest, taught by his father. He was a priest-in-training, who was making his first solo sacrifice. The timing is then when Cain had reached the age of accountability to the LORD.

---

4 *And Abel, he also brought of the firstlings of his flock and of the fat thereof. And the LORD had respect unto Abel and to his offering;*

ד וְהֶ֨בֶל הֵבִ֥יא גַם־ה֛וּא מִבְּכֹר֥וֹת צֹאנ֖וֹ וּמֵֽחֶלְבֵהֶ֑ן וַיִּ֣שַׁע יְהוָ֔ה אֶל־הֶ֖בֶל וְאֶל־מִנְחָתֽוֹ.

D1 Abel come also he firstborn flock fat portions to look YHWH towards Abel towards offering.

Verse four does not mention any further passage of time, relative to verse three. It instead begins by stating that Abel would "come also." This then links Abel with Cain, as far as being prepared to perform the priestly functions that came with time and experience. This is another clue that the two sons are twins,

The Cain & Abel Story

born on the same day, meaning the timing of verse three applies to both. Therefore, they both will come of age at the same time.

The time of the first fruits and the firstlings of the flock can be seen as late spring, after growth has reappeared on the earth. Regardless of the exact time, it could be that Cain's collection of his efforts occurred first, and then Abel's sacrifice of the firstborn followed at a later time during the same season. It makes sense that the ceremony was not a private affair. Adam, Eve, and each brother would have been in attendance at each ceremony, probably with a feast afterwards so the cooked offerings could be consumed. In this way, everyone would witness how YAHWEH responded to each offering.

In this scenario, it makes sense that there was only one altar built and used. It would have been built by Adam and represented the family "temple." Because there was a set time each year for the first fruits and the fat of firstlings to be available, everything could be brought to a central location. That would be where all offerings were presented to the LORD. It may have been a result of trial and error over the years, which determined the produce of the plants would be offered before the fat of the lambs.

In the case of a sacrificial animal being burnt, the heat would cause the "fat portions" (*cheleb* - וְהֶבְלְחֵמוּ) to drip into the burning wood, making the flames rise higher. That is what happens on a barbecue grill, and lamb is especially fatty. A prepared carcass would be placed on a spit, such that the fat would be attached to the meat. The fat would burn, sending a smoke rising for YAHWEH, leaving the cooked meat within the charred remains. That would be eaten later.

A raging fire, aided by fat drippings, would make plants and fruits burn completely, sending off smoke but leaving uneatable

Chapter 2: The purpose of Cain and Abel

remains. By offering them first, over a lower flame, they could keep them eatable, but with a less pleasing smoke produced. Even then, they would have to remain over fire for a shorter period of time. Their preparation would mean burning more chaff and husk, and less pulp of the fruits and vegetables.

It could be presumed that the first priests lived more on the fruits, berries, nuts, grains, and vegetables, on a day-to-day basis, with animals killed for their meat only consumed at ritualistic events. Animals would be raised for wool, milk, and things derived from milk. As such, the offering of the first fruits would have less significance, as the plant would not lose its life to give up its seed. The killing of an animal, which had a way of communicating with Adam, and probably Abel too, as well as a relationship to the animal's mother, would have been a much more traumatic act. All of this must be seen as relevant to everyone involved.

Prior to the birth of two sons to Adam, Adam would have been solely responsible for all sacrifices made to the LORD. If his experience, including those times he made burnt offerings while assisted by his sons, the end result would have always been YAHWEH "looking towards his offering," or showing Adam "respect," then it might have been assumed that YAHWEH was pleased with both the offering of plants and animals. Because verse four says that the LORD looked at the sacrifice of Abel, which was a sign of respect, and that is not stated about Cain's offering, one must presume YAHWEH had a reason greater than a dislike for vegetables.

The point of this nonrecognition by YAHWEH upon Cain is hugely important to grasp. It becomes the root cause of the actions taken by Cain. One has to ask, "Why would YAHWEH look at Abel's sacrifice and not Cain's?" "Why would YAH-

The Cain & Abel Story

WEH respect the burnt fat of firstlings and not the burnt plants and fruits of Cain's garden?"

While the answer is not stated, one has to be able to see the relevance of the sacrifice of a life to God as being more important than the sacrifice of "fruit." By definition, "fruit" is "the ripened ovary or ovaries of a seed-bearing plant." That means that the yield of a crop is feminine in essence, as males do not have ovaries. Additionally, "fruit" is representative of "an edible, usually sweet and fleshy form of" a plant, and not typically the whole of it, including root and stem. Offering fruit means a whole entity is not sacrificed. The use of "fruit" implies the plant may still be growing and able to produce more fruit. It makes sense that the LORD would be more attentive to the sacrifice of a whole life, than to a part of a life form.

As that perspective needs to be viewed, I believe there is a more direct explanation as to why God would look at the burnt offering of the fat of a firstling and not look upon the offering of fruit. It has nothing to do with a judgment by God, as one being better than the other. It has only to do with one offering being to God the Father and the other not.

Because Abel sacrificed an air-breathing animal, whose life breath came from God, the animal thus had a soul and the LORD looked at the soul being released. It was YAHWEH's responsibility as the Father to receive back that soul. Cain was not making an offering of an air-breathing entity; but instead, he offered the bounty of growth that actually helped create the air breathed. Thus, YAHWEH did not look with respect on Cain's sacrifice, simply because that offering was not the responsibility of the LORD, the Father.

That responsibility fell to the Mother, who is the Earth, the goddess who joined with the Father to make all life on our

Chapter 2: The purpose of Cain and Abel

planet. The land is governed by the Earth Mother and it brings forth its fruit and harvest with her blessings. Therefore, Cain was making a sacrifice that would have pleased the Earth, as it represented the fruits she had bestowed to him.

While the Earth goddess deserved honorable recognition, Adam had told his sons they were priests of the LORD YAHWEH and they should make ritual offering to that God. Therefore, God did not look at Cain's offering because it was not a proper sacrifice worthy of the LORD's respect (i.e.: His looking upon it).

In a way, the combination of two offerings, as one whole recognition of the LORD, is like God telling Adam that he will have dominion over Eve. While not a direct disrespect of the wife-to-be, the mother in waiting, it states the two of them are one in relationship with God. Adam serves the LORD, and Eve serves Adam. Likewise, the Earth goddess serve YAHWEH, and like all the angels of the LORD, the Earth is to serve mankind. Therefore, the bounty of the earth is ultimately an indirect blessing of God, while a direct blessing of the Earth Mother. An offering that thanks her deity is seen by YAHWEH as His due, but not His primary demand.

As a priest for the One God, no others gods are to be honored by His people - Adam and sons. All of the lesser gods either used mankind or abused mankind, at that point in the earth's early history. Mankind feared the gods, as primitive beings that only recognized mysterious powers they needed to appease. Adam and Eve knew God personally, as their Father. God did not create Adam and Eve to populate the world with more of the same fear of the ethereal. Since YAHWEH has dominion over the Earth and all others gods and goddesses, there was no reason for Adam to honor any other god.

The Cain & Abel Story

Adam had taught his sons to build an altar and to sacrifice a young (thus pure) living animal to the LORD. The fact that Abel raised the flock, and not Cain, was no excuse for Cain not to offer a life to the LORD, if two separate offerings were expecting two separate blessings. It was Cain's responsibility to offer fruits to Abel, in trade for another of Abel's firstling, which Cain could then sacrifice to YAHWEH. Only that would draw the attention of the LORD; but that obviously was not clearly known by Adam and sons at the time of this learning experience (more trial and error training).

One can further assume that Adam played a role in allowing his sons to make mistakes, as the role of a father is to teach the children, through lessons, that life is hard. You learn from mistakes, and some mistakes can be very hurtful. It may be that Adam was learning something new at the same time.

As the story goes further, one can assume that both Adam and Eve loved their sons and wanted the best for them. One would expect that Adam and Eve attempted to console Cain, much like parents try to encourage their children in sports, after they feel the pain of a loss. Still, as the son and daughter of the LORD, they knew that YAHWEH would teach their sons best. The fact that the LORD speaks to Cain is evidence that the whole family had the Grand Father watching over them. While they could not see YAHWEH, they could hear Him.

---

5 *but unto Cain and to his offering He had not respect. And Cain was very wroth, and his countenance fell.*

ה וְאֶל-קַיִן וְאֶל-מִנְחָתוֹ, לֹא שָׁעָה; וַיִּחַר לְקַיִן מְאֹד, וַיִּפְּלוּ פָּנָיו.

Chapter 2: The purpose of Cain and Abel

H1 *Towards Cain toward offering not to look became angry Cain abundance to fall face.*

This tells of the emotional response Cain had when his sacrifice was not respected by YAHWEH. We now learn that the LORD did not look upon Cain's offering, meaning no respect was paid to his first fruits. This means that a sign of God occurred after Abel's offering, but the same sign did not occur after Cain's. Assuming that both used the same altar, the lack of a sign after Cain made his offering could only have caused him to wait and see the result of his brother's sacrifice.

Because that result implied YAHWEH was not pleased with Cain's presentation, his inner being seethed with anger. At first, this anger was withheld from expression. There may have been celebration for Abel's blessing, of which Cain had to act as if he were as pleased as Adam and Eve, but inside he was upset. After a while, this inner rage became apparent in his outer being, when he wore his emotions on his face.

The Hebrew word "*panim*" ("וַיִּפְּלוּ") actually states "faces," in the plural. This means that not only was the emotional disturbance within Cain apparent on his face, it was obvious as each family member came to him. Cain clearly showed his dissatisfaction with the lack of respect God showed towards him. A scowl was probably quite evident, but his body language would also show that inner rage.

The word "*panim*" can also translate as "anger, appearance, attitude, favor, condition, honor, humiliation, shame," and "direction" (as well as many others). This was to become present in "abundance," as "very wroth" means. Cain was, therefore, not unlike any of us who has been faced with rejection and shame,

The Cain & Abel Story

such that an inner anger causes emotional outbursts. Cain could have acted out his frustrations, taking apart the altar, or kicking a stack of wood or fruits. This verse lets the reader know that Cain could not control his inner emotions.

The most important word to understand here is "וַיִּפְּלוּ" ("*way·yip·pə·lū*"), which is a form of "לִפְנַי" ("*naphal*"), stating "fell," as the past tense of "to fall." It is one thing to read this word and imagine Cain turning a smile into a frown, or having a "long face," but the point is to see how the whole of Cain, in all of his "countenance" and "demeanor," began a downward spiral. He was literally and figuratively "fallen," as his despair had curled him up on the ground, with his face in the dirt.

---

6 *And the LORD said unto Cain: 'Why art thou wroth? and why is thy countenance fallen?*

וַיֹּאמֶר יְהוָה, אֶל-קָיִן: לָמָּה חָרָה לָךְ, וְלָמָּה נָפְלוּ פָנֶיךָ.

V1 *To say YHWH towards Cain what burns you with anger which to fall face?*

This verse is making a statement that the LORD held no ill-will towards Cain because of Cain not making a sacrifice to Him. YAHWEH is concerned about Cain's demeanor, both his inner heart (the emotional center) and his outer body (his actions of rage). Thus, God speaks to Cain in an effort to calm him down, so He can offer some Grand Fatherly advice, of a spiritual nature.

The LORD asked Cain, "What makes you burn with anger?"

Chapter 2: The purpose of Cain and Abel

This is not a question that God wants to have answered, as God knows all. God knew full well why Cain was angry. The question was for Cain's benefit, for Cain to answer. God knew Cain needed to come to his senses and begin to realize his anger was misdirected and rooted in self. Cain's anger was because he was jealous that his brother got recognition and he did not. The LORD asked Cain if he knew a human flaw is letting one's emotions control one's thoughts. Unchecked emotions allow a brain to go wild with imaginary thoughts.

The LORD then asked another question to Cain, "Why has your appearance changed?" Again, this is not because YAHWEH did not know Cain's heart and mind, but the question was posed for Cain to realize the answer. Cain's inner rage had caused his internal system to react accordingly, so it ceased to elevate Cain's spirit. Cain had fallen low in spirits.

A priest should reflect an elevated state of being, due to dedication to the LORD and the benefits the LORD returns in kind. Cain's outer actions, the look on his face, the words he spews, and the things he takes his frustrations out on are likewise lowering his energy. Cain was not taking the high road, but was taking the road away from his upbringing. He was rebelling against everyone and everything and making it difficult for others to help him, including YAHWEH.

The questions posed by the LORD need to be answered by Cain. It is up to him to get control over himself. Cain must be able to "step outside himself" and be able to see how others see him. If Cain could recall how he has seen others lose control of their actions, due to emotional imbalances, Cain could assess his own actions from a logical perspective. He could realize how childish he was acting and how such actions will pass with time, if he could listen to the voice of reason.

The Cain & Abel Story

7 *If thou doest well, shall it not be lifted up? and if thou doest not well, sin croucheth at the door; and unto thee is its desire, but thou mayest rule over it.'*

ז הֲלוֹא אִם-תֵּיטִיב, שְׂאֵת, וְאִם לֹא תֵיטִיב, לַפֶּתַח חַטָּאת רֹבֵץ; וְאֵלֶיךָ, תְּשׁוּקָתוֹ, וְאַתָּה, תִּמְשָׁל-בּוֹ.

Z1 *Not if to be good dignity if not to be good opening sin stretch oneself out towards a longing you have dominion over.*

The questions posed by YAHWEH were not answered, which implies Cain was unresponsive. Next, the LORD asked Cain to ponder his past experiences, and think of times when he was rewarded. YAHWEH asked Cain, "Haven't you found high spirits within you when you have done well?" God's question was a recommendation that history contains the answers.

The LORD tells Cain of his known history, such that when Cain has done good, in his thoughts and deeds and through his well behavior, then he has been rewarded by uplifted spirits. This means Cain's emotional state had, at a previous time, been elevated by God's presence in his heart. All Cain needed to do was duplicate a scenario where he does something that is good. God is attempting to entice Cain to do something positive, because his negative reaction has made him lose control of his emotions, causing his spirit to become deflated.

This suggests to Cain that if his intent was to please YAHWEH through a living sacrifice, then he should come up with a way that does that. Since an offering of plants and their fruits

Chapter 2: The purpose of Cain and Abel

did not bring the attention of the LORD, then Cain simply has to do what Abel did. However, if Cain refuses to realize he has made the mistake, his own error in judgment, then Cain will continue to have his spirits fall, to the point that he opens a door for sin to reach his ear.

At this point, recall that the punishment given the serpent, when it was banished from Heaven. The serpent lost its arms and legs (or four legs), causing it to forever have to slither on the ground. With the use of legs, it was able to raise itself somehow, to gain equal height to the face of Eve (and Adam). It was raised to the level of the head, able to influence Adam and Eve by getting into their minds via their ears. God's punishment was to lower the serpent, the most crafty of God's animal creations, to the ground. There no one's ear could hear the influences of the serpent, unless one wallowed on the ground where the snake dwells.

The LORD was explaining that to Cain. Cain had not acted as a priest to YAHWEH in the offering of plants to God the Father. An offering that honored Earth the Mother could not be looked upon by God. That act would be a sign of disrespect to the Earth. A gift of the physical realm can only honor the goddess of that realm. YAHWEH, the One God of the spiritual realm of most importance, the giver of life on Earth, the Creator of babies in the womb, and the protector of all air-breathing life, He was the reason for the ceremony of offering.

God told Cain (in essence), "If you cling to the earth as your god, you will never do well in My eyes." The LORD said, "If you remain on the ground for long, then you open the door for the serpent to influence you to do greater sins." Those were warnings that came from God out of love for Cain. However, Cain was the one who ultimately had to make his own choices,

The Cain & Abel Story

and determine whom he would serve as a priest.

As this conversation with YAHWEH concludes, the LORD reminds Cain of the gift of free will. God tells Cain, "You can rule over yourself, rather than let some influence for evil rule over you." This is the same state that existed when Adam and Eve were in Heaven with YAHWEH. God told them they could eat anything EXCEPT one fruit. God did not place bars and walls around the tree of knowledge of good and evil. Adam and Eve had dominion over themselves and were allowed to choose to do right, based on one rule.

Cain was no different than his parents. Cain could chose to obey the LORD and do well as a servant to Him (a priest). Or, he could turn away from God and serve the enticements of another master, in the material realm.

The LORD told Cain that the desire of sin was to slither over to him. In his lowered position, he invited that visit. Satan was "longing," and full of "desire" to get a chance to bring evil upon another of God's children.

The LORD knew the gift of craftiness given to the serpent was irresistible to human beings, even those born of God (heroes, with immortality as long as they are sin free). The LORD knew the serpent would trick Eve, and thus Adam, causing them to sin. God knew his children needed to sin so He could send them to earth with a purpose, to become earthly priests with knowledge of YAHWEH and goodness.

They were to also know of the serpent and sin. The warning YAHWEH gave to Cain, that the desire of Satan would soon become Cain's desire if Cain laid in a position of subservience to sin (Satan), was based on the future known by God. Cain was known to become the first failed priest, one of many who would follow. Cain would serve YAHWEH indirectly, by taking the

Chapter 2: The purpose of Cain and Abel

knowledge of God and an acknowledgement of sin to a world that knew nothing of either.

Chapter 3

The sin of Cain

8 *And Cain spoke unto Abel his brother. And it came to pass, when they were in the field, that Cain rose up against Abel his brother, and slew him.*

ח וַיֹּאמֶר קַיִן אֶל-הֶבֶל אָחִיו, וַיְהִי בִּהְיוֹתָם בַּשָּׂדֶה, וַיָּקָם קַיִן אֶל-הֶבֶל אָחִיו, וַיַּהַרְגֵהוּ.

Ch1 *To say Cain towards Abel brother to come to pass to be field to arise Cain towards Abel brother to kill.*

We are now led from the advice of YAHWEH to Cain to a subsequent conversation between Cain and Abel. The unwritten conversation is the one that took place between sin (the serpent) and Cain, while Cain was wallowing on the ground, in low spirits. One can assume that evil had influenced Cain to confront his brother, such that the words that Cain spoke to Abel were not

Chapter 3: The sin of Cain

from love (a high spirit emotion). Although Cain could have approached Abel in a calm and civil approach, that would have been as a deception.

While not knowing the exact topic of conversation between Cain and Abel, we do know that anger was inside Cain and he was angry because the LORD respected Abel's offering, but not Cain's. If Cain had been influenced by the crafty serpent, as often is the case, Cain may have come upon Abel as though he had gotten over his anger, in order to approach Abel without causing him to be defensive. A direct verbal assault would have caused Abel to seek help, knowing God would answer his call if Adam was out of earshot.

It may be that Cain approached Abel about a trade for the next ritual sacrifice to the LORD, asking Abel what it would cost for a yearling. Whatever the conversation, Cain left Abel without doing him harm, because the next statement says more time passed afterwards. The passing of time could have been leaving the conversation with agreed upon plans for the next ritual rite of spring, the following year. However, that much time would not be in Cain's plans, for he would return to catch his brother off guard.

In this passing of time, one may gain some insight from the Palestinian version of this story, the brothers named Kabil and Habil. In that story, the conversation Kabil (Cain) had with Habil (Abel) was a stated threat on Abel's life, at which point Abel responded with a promise to defend himself and slay Cain. That story says Abel was stronger than Cain and could have easily defeated Cain in a fight. Cain does not know what method he should use to kill Abel, meaning a period of time passed as Cain plotted revenge.

During this time, the Palestinian mythology says that the devil

The Cain & Abel Story

appeared to Cain in human form. The devil called upon a crow to lite before him. Once the bird was rested, the devil crushed its head between two stones. In an Armenian (Turkish) version of this story, Satan took the form of a raven and challenged another raven to battle, with the evil raven holding a sharp rock (called a "pointed black pebble") in its beak. The Satan raven slit the throat of the other raven, killing it. With that act done, Satan dropped the rock and Cain picked it up, hiding it in his girdle. The Armenians still call a piece of flint rock "Satan's nails," due to this story.[1]

Regardless of how much time passed and how Cain actually killed Abel, it is safe to assume there was a period of time when he plotted Abel's death. This passing of time is what indicated an act of premeditated murder and not a crime of passion. Cain has plenty of time to recover from whatever insecurities he felt from YAHWEH not looking upon his offering with respect; instead, as time passed, Cain maintained his anger.

In the continuation of verse eight, the Hebrew word "*sadeh*" is used ("הַשָּׂדֶה" – "*besadeh*"), which means, "field, country, land, soil, ground," and even "battlefield." While one can see this as indicative of the landscape upon which sheep and cattle would graze, that would be better stated as "pasture ground" (the Hebrew words "*na-ah*" – "נֹאאן" or "*mir-eh*" – "הַעֲרָמ*.*" Thus, a "field" better represents an area where crops are grown. Seeing that setting would then indicate that Abel was drawn into the land set aside for Cain to cultivate crops, such as corn, wheat, or perhaps hay, which would be used to feed animals during the winter. Cain could have used an enticement to Abel, such as, "Come see what I have to offer in the fields, as trade for a firstling."

---

1   An article entitled *Cain and Abel* a listing under "scriptures and legends selected and edited by D. L. Ashliman." http://www.pitt.edu/~dash/cain.html

Chapter 3: The sin of Cain

In something like a cornfield, or sunflower field, or any field where the crops grow high enough to conceal an act of crime, this could be the scene that is set up. Cain could have staged rocks that would be used to pummel Abel, within the rows of plants, where he would have led Abel. He could have hidden a sharp flint in his clothing, with the plants hiding his reaching for a weapon. Certainly, if his plan was successful, tall plants would conceal the dead body of his brother.

When one gets to the Hebrew word "*qom*" ("סָקָם" – "*wa-ya-qom*"), which primarily means, "to arise, to stand up," or "to rise," we see that Cain was in a figurative state of lowness, as pointed out by YAHWEH, with the emotions required to kill one's brother then becoming raised. Still, Cain was also in a literal state of crouching, as if lying in wait, ready to pounce on Abel. This sets up a scene where Cain led Abel into a field of tall plants, and then hid low as he maneuvered into his strategic position to strike. In both cases, we see that Cain was under the influence of sin, as warned against by God, then rose up against his brother and killed him.

Recalling Genesis 3, when Eve was influenced to sin by the serpent; she was told, "you will be like God" if you sin and break the rule of the LORD. Imagine Cain hearing a similar argument, where he was told he will be able to elevate above his brother Abel, like a god, thus he would believe he was able to arise like YAHWEH. The LORD had been summoned to the sacrifices that were made, so God could look with respect upon the actions of His priests, from above. Now, Cain was able to disrespect Abel from this advantage point.

In the midst of the fruits of Cain's labors, he would sacrifice his brother to his pleasure. Cain would look upon his killing as if Abel were sacrificed so that Cain could be godlike. His think-

The Cain & Abel Story

ing might have been along the line, "If YAHWEH looks upon the offering of a lamb with respect, then He will love my offering of this pet of the LORD."

Since time had passed, and this event is at some time after Cain felt anger by not having YAHWEH look upon his offering, it makes sense that Cain was no longer in a state of rage. With the passage of time, open wounds begin to heal, so Cain was not out of control when he killed Abel. His act was one purely motivated by revenge, where Cain wanted others to feel the pain he felt.

This would not be Abel, as his body would feel nothing after death, and Adam and Eve would have been feeling both pain and happiness over one son's reward and the other's lack. They would not be deserving of one's vengeance. Cain wanted YAHWEH to feel the loss of the priest whom he favored. Cain wanted the LORD to feel remorse for having pushed Cain to that point of evil. However, all of that intent, motivated by revenge, would do nothing but cause Cain to fall further.

His new sin would bring about a heightening of his remorse. Whatever pleasure might have come from killing was surely fleeting. Cain had probably not had the foresight to plan what to do with a dead body, nor how to act around his grieving parents. Cain would have instantly felt his conscience shaking his muscles, with his inner voice asking him, "What have you done?" Thus, Satan had tricked another of God's human beings into a life of misery.

---

9 *And the LORD said unto Cain: 'Where is Abel thy brother?' And he said: 'I know not; am I my brother's keeper?'*

Chapter 3: The sin of Cain

ט .יִכְנָא יִחְא רְמֶשָׁה, יִתְּעְדָיָ אל רְמָאיִנ; דִּיחְא לבֵהֶ יאֵ, וְיִק-לאֶ הנְהִי רְמָאיִנ.

T1 *To say YHWH towards Cain where Abel brother? To say not to know to watch a brother I.*

Again, we have YAHWEH asking Cain a rhetorical question, one which the LORD knows the answer full well. The point of God asking, "Where is your brother?" is to ask the fooled Cain if his godlike state has made him all-knowing. Cain's response is that he does not know where Abel's soul is, although he knows where his dead body lies. Just as Adam and Eve felt ashamed and naked after they sinned, Cain is likewise scared and vulnerable.

The point of a question also serves the purpose of showing that Abel's body is not in the open where he can easily be spotted when he is missed. The death will cause the need for a search. The terrain in which Abel herded his flocks was open, but wide ranging. With cliffs, crevasses, and dangerous inclines part of the landscape, Abel could have fallen in an accident while looking for a stray from his flock. Since the fields of crops are in full growth following the time of the first fruits, Abel's body could not be easily found within the rows. Adam and Eve would not expect their first born son to have killed his brother. Thus, the LORD is echoing the cries of Cain's parents to Cain.

Cain denies knowing anything about the whereabouts of Abel. He has followed the sin of murder with the sin of lying. When Adam and Eve were caught in hiding, after their sin, they admitted their wrong-doing, while doing some finger pointing at who influenced who.

When Adam had sinned and God asked him, "Where are

The Cain & Abel Story

you?" (Again knowing full well where Adam was), Adam answered YAHWEH by saying, "I heard you in the garden, and I was afraid because I was naked; so I hid." Adam and Eve had sinned and felt guilt, but they did not compound their sin by lying to God. Cain, on the other hand, thinking he had become godlike, answered the LORD with a lie, saying, "I don't know."

Cain is not going to stop sinning, because when he lies to the LORD he becomes bolder. He acted as if he were God's equal by mocking YAHWEH, asking a question in response. Cain tried to turn the table on God, by retorting, "Am I my brother's keeper?"

In Genesis 4, verse two, after we know of Abel's birth, we then are told that Abel was a keeper of flocks. The Hebrew word "*ra'ah*" ("הָעֵר") was used there. Here, the word "*shamar*" ("רְמֵשֹׁה" – "*hasamer*") is found, which has the same meaning. Abel was the keeper of flocks, not Cain. Cain is now asking if he has been anointed as the one "having charge of," as an "overseer," or if he was then a "watchman." That is the responsibility of a shepherd, much more than a farmer needs to watch plants grow.

In one way, Cain acted as if his realm was over plants, those which YAHWEH would not look upon with respect. Cain was not given the responsibility of watching over Abel, because he was not a trained shepherd. Cain is then using sarcasm to imply that the LORD might find pleasure in Cain's offering of Abel, if Cain had been given that work earlier. As it was, Cain was just a lowly farmer who watched over nothing and got no respect from God. So, Cain was flippantly telling YAHWEH, "Why would I know anything? I am not good enough to watch over air-breathing creatures."

The word "*shamar*" also bears the meaning, "to preserve,"

Chapter 3: The sin of Cain

which states the necessity to watch over something that does not stay in one place all the time. A shepherd is one who preserves, like a father does his children. Children need someone nearby to save them from wandering into dangerous situation. In a world where mortal dangers were ever present, it was ultimately up to God "to preserve" all life. This is why a priest is called a shepherd, and why the LORD sent Adam to tend to the human flock that roamed without one to preserve them.

YAHWEH had demonstrated his overseeing of Cain, when God saw Cain's countenance had fallen. The LORD acted to preserve Cain's life by telling him he was in danger of letting sin influence him. Therefore, Cain was lashing out at God by saying God was the responsible party who dropped the ball.

In a way, Cain was making it seem that Abel should have been doing his job (and not visiting Cain's fields) watching his flocks, while YAHWEH was watching over him. It was the LORD's responsibility to preserve Abel. Cain could not have that responsibility and tend to his plants somewhere else.

Chapter 4

The initial punishment of Cain

10 *And He said: 'What hast thou done? the voice of thy brother's blood crieth unto Me from the ground.*

י הָמָדֲאָה-ןִמ יַלֵא םיִקֲעֹצ ,ךיִחָא יֵמְּד לוֹק ;ָתיִׂשָע הֶמ ,רֶמאֹּיַו.

Y1 *To say what accomplish? Voice blood brother to call out towards from ground!*

Following Cain's flippant attitude towards YAHWEH, Cain is asked another question, one that causes Cain's mind to open and understand what he has done. The LORD knows full well what actions have been committed by Cain, so his question is more of a command for Cain to ask himself the question. That represents the time when Cain realized his crime could not be hidden, nor go unpunished.

When verse 10 says, "the voice of thy brother's blood cries

Chapter 4: The initial punishment of Cain

out to me from the ground," especially following the question posed by YAHWEH, it becomes the voice of Abel asking the question. It is the LORD becoming Abel's voice, as Abel is speaking to YAHWEH. As soon as Abel died his soul was with the LORD, so there was no need for any voice to come from the ground. Abel was dead, so he was not still trapped in his body, nor was his spilled blood pleading for help. The voice of Abel was with YAHWEH in spirit.

The use of "blood" ("*dǝ·mê* " - "יְמֵי") is both a statement of Cain and Abel sharing the same genes, the same lineage, and a statement of the form of death, where blood being spilled would indicate the use of a weapon. Not only were Cain and Abel brothers, they were the grandchildren of YAHWEH, because He is the Father of Adam and Eve. God has a special link to that bloodline, so the LORD must let Cain know the crime will not go unknown. The use of a weapon, such as a blunt object (rock or log) or a sharp object (flint edge), would indicate murder, as bleeding would come from an attack. Still, there is a more significant meaning that connects this verse to the rest in this series, as well as the previous chapters and verses leading up to this point.

The "voice," from the Hebrew word "*qol*" ("לוֹק"), is not only an audible utterance from a human being. It also states the projection of an "outcry," or "report." It represents "news, crying," and that there was a "witness" to the crime, who spoke out for the dead Abel. That "voice" comes "from the ground," "from the land," "from the dust," "from the fields," "from the soil," and thus, "from Mother Earth." She is the grandmother of Abel, as the mother of Adam and Eve. Thus, the Earth goddess also shares a link with the "blood" spilled.

As all living beings are born of the union between the mate-

The Cain & Abel Story

rial (Earth) and the spiritual (God), the death of a living creature is mourned by the essential mother. The "blood" that has been spilt includes the evidence of that union, on a biological level. The earthy-physical traits form the body, with the spirit of God controlling the biological processes. It is the LORD Eve thanked when Cain was born, because God separated and rejoined the DNA held in the union of egg and sperm. God split the cells of the bodies he formed within the womb; and then He breathed life into an organism that exited from Eve's embryonic fluids. This is how mortals cycle through life and death, and why YAHWEH told Adam his fate was that of a mortal man:

> "By the sweat of your brow you will eat your food until you return to the ground, since from it you were taken; for dust you are and to dust you will return." (Genesis 3:19)

This shows both the love of God in Heaven and the Mother earth from whose womb we all come, as physical entities on her plane. Her love causes her voice to be heard, as she cries out to her LORD, YAHWEH. It is a repeated symbolism in the Holy Bible, where Mary the Mother of Jesus was with him at the cross, witnessing his blood being spilled on the ground. It is a theme depicted in religious art, from the Madonna with child, to the Madonna holding the lifeless body of her son. Abel had come from dust and returned to it, causing the dust mother to cry. Because Abel was murdered, the Earth mother lifted her voice to the LORD for justice.

One must realize this connection because Cain, as the first born son of Adam and Eve, would become a tiller of the ground. He would cultivate the earth and bring forth its bounty. The punishment YAHWEH placed upon Adam was:

> "Cursed is the ground because of you; through

Chapter 4: The initial punishment of Cain

painful toil you will eat food from it all the days
of your life. It will produce thorns and thistles
for you, and you will eat the plants of the field."
(Genesis 3:17-18)

For that reason, Cain was dedicated to be a servant to the Earth Goddess. Cain would then be able to do the work Adam had to do, to make it much easier to stay alive and care for his family. The name "Cain" means "Stalk" or "Reed," where there is inference to herbs growing. Additionally, as a verb, it means "Acquire" and "Create," which is in honor of one who will follow in his father's footsteps, as a worker of the ground, but with greater ease. The Earth Mother will bless the dedication of Cain to her, by turning her soft and nurturing side to Cain's plough.

From this understanding, one is able to see the urgency of Cain realizing the impact of the question, "What have you done?" By killing his brother and spilling Abel's blood on the Earth goddess, the one to whom he was dedicated, and the one who blessed him, Cain knew his act did more harm to himself. Cain had made his ally cry out to YAHWEH for vengeance against him.

---

11 *And now cursed art thou from the ground, which hath opened her mouth to receive thy brother's blood from thy hand.*

אי הַתְּעַן, רוּרָא הַתָּא, ומִ-הַמָדָאֲה רְשֶׁא הַתְצְפּ תֶא-פיָה, הַתַחַמַל תֶא-תָמֵי
הַחיִ מָיָדָדְ.

A2 *Now to curse you from earth who to open her mouth to take the lifeblood brother hand.*

The Cain & Abel Story

YAHWEH next told Cain just how deep a hole he had gotten himself into. While Adam and Eve had broken the only rule set by YAHWEH, it was up to God to punish them. Adam was told, "cursed is the ground" (" *'ă·rū·rāh hā·'ă·ḏā·māh* " – "אֲרוּרָה הָאֲדָמָה"). whereas Cain was told, "are cursed you from the earth" ("*'ā·rūr 'at·tāh min-hā·'ă·ḏā·māh*" – "הָאֲדָמָה מִן־ אַתָּה אָרוּר"). This means Cain's curse was not from YAHWEH. Instead, he was cursed by Mother Earth. For her to have supported Cain as one dedicated to her, to have him disgrace her through spilling the blood of a human life, she now removes her blessing and turns it to a curse.

The relationship between YAHWEH and the mother of Adam and Eve was no different than the relationship she has with all living creatures on earth. All are physical entities (earthly), while all are living through the presence of a soul (heavenly). Thus, any spilling of blood would have caused the same reaction, just as all death still calls upon the LORD to accept the soul back and the Earth to receive back the body (ashes to ashes, dust to dust).

This means an offering of the firstlings would have created a cry from the Earth goddess, if the animal had been sacrificed in the open, allowing its blood pour onto the ground. This curse is then a statement about the sanctity of an altar, such that it had to be constructed in a way so blood did not dishonor the Earth goddess. The act of blood offerings meant the collection of blood in some reservoir made of stone or earthenware. Those who worshipped the *elohim*, or the immortals created by YAHWEH when he created the heavens, would find the use of blood in their rituals important. This can be explained as a way of avoiding a curse from the Earth goddess.

Chapter 4: The initial punishment of Cain

It is also important to realize that Adam and Eve were not the first human beings on planet earth. The births of Cain and Abel did not bring the total number of human beings to four. Man and woman were created on the "sixth day," where "day" is not six rotations of the earth, but six phases of God's work. This length of time is unfathomable in terms of time understood by human brains. This means that many ages and evolutions of mankind have occurred around the world; and in that process, many living creatures have died, with their blood spilt on the ground. However, Adam and Eve were the first priests to YAHWEH, with their sons also priests.

Cain was a priest to YAHWEH but he had been dedicated to the Earth goddess, for the purpose of obtaining her blessings. Cain's offering to YAHWEH was not looked upon because it was a sacrifice only for the eyes of the Earth. As a priest, a sacrifice of a living creature needed to take place on an altar, so the blood would be consumed by the flames and become transformed into a pleasing sense to the LORD. To make a living sacrifice upon the plain ground would be seen by the Earth goddess as obscene and as disgraceful as are the ordinary disrespect of life, held by a more animal-type man. The actions of early man were more often than not influenced by sin, as reactions to an emotional imbalance: fear, rage, survival, etc. Thus, for Cain to act as a priest and sacrifice his brother to the LORD, but spill his blood on the ground, not an altar, he was deemed unpriestly and sinful. On all such mortal acts, the Earth places a curse.

---

12 *When thou tillest the ground, it shall not henceforth yield unto thee her strength; a fugitive and a wanderer shalt thou be in the earth.*

The Cain & Abel Story

וְרָאָב הָיְתָה, דְּנָן עֵן; דְּלְ הִחָל-תֵּה וְסֵת-אל, הַמָּדָאָה-תֵא דבֹעַת יִכְ **בִי**.

B2 *When to work the earth not to add to give strength to quiver to wander to become earth.*

This verse restates what Cain was trained to do, as his vocation. Verse 2 ends by saying, "Cain was a tiller of the ground" ("*obed adamah*" – "to work ground"), and verse 12 now begins by referencing that position as farmer, saying "When you work the land" ("*eth hadamah*"). This means that Cain was a farmer, in the sense that he worked the land occupied by Adam, east of Eden. As an assistant to Adam, Cain was trained to grow crops in established fields. The land was made hard for Adam, due to his sin and punishment, in the sense that heavenly soil requires no toil to plant. Working the earth outside of Eden brought sweat to the brow, and that is why Adam's first son would become his helper. Cain's birth would ease Adam's burden. However, once Cain had sinned against Mother Earth, his punishment was worse than Adam's.

This punishment was not the result of YAHWEH ordering the Earth to shun Cain and make her surface hard for Cain to work. It was the Earth Mother's punishment for having been disgraced and defiled. The LORD saw that punishment as just; and He told Cain what his punishment would be, so there would be no argument. That punishment meant Cain could no longer stay in one place to farm. It meant he would forever be sentenced to move to places where crops grew naturally, plentiful enough for him to forage. Since his presence would cause the ground to grow hard, killing natural vegetation, Cain would have to always keep mov-

Chapter 4: The initial punishment of Cain

ing to the next point of survival.

It is worthy to note that Cain's survival needs had changed. He no longer could depend on his skills of labor. Instead, Cain would have to rely on his cunning abilities. This is a sign of one dedicated to the serpent, the animal YAHWEH had made the most crafty. This could mean that Cain would occasionally run across a field cultivated by another human being, where he could either steal food or make pleas for handouts. Due to Cain's hero status, as able to outlive mere mortals, he could have used that as trade for his necessities for daily living. This type of encounter with other human beings would then be, in time, how Cain would to find a wife.

No matter where Cain would go, he would never be able to work the fields again. His success had been due to the blessing of the Earth goddess, because Adam dedicated his first born son to her. With the spillage of blood on her soil, she would never again lend her strength to Cain.

That became a life sentence for murder, with Cain still a young man, as far as heroes go. The lives of Seth and the others in the line of Adam were generally over 900 years. There is nothing stated that would indicate Cain would have a shorter life span. Since his sentence occurred after Cain and Abel's first official sacrifices to YAHWEH, they were probably around 140 to 160 years of age. Based on a 10x rule of thumb, Cain would have been the human equivalent of a young teen, 14-16 years old. Cain, as the son of the Son of God (Adam), would face the equivalent of a 800 year sentence, or about having to serve 80 years today.

---

13 *And Cain said unto the LORD: 'My punishment is greater than I*

The Cain & Abel Story

can bear.

גי רמאיּו, ןיִק לֶא-הָוהְי: לוֹדָגּ יִנוֲֺע ,אֹשְּׂנִמ.

G2 *To say Cain towards YHWH great punishment for inequity to carry!*

In one sense, this verse can be read as Cain being flabbergasted at his punishment for killing his brother and spilling his blood on the Earth. However, there is a more important way to read the words written.

Before Cain knew the punishment for the sin he had committed, he was acting as if he were under the influence of evil, thinking he was a god, an equal to YAHWEH. After the LORD had exposed how Cain's resentment, jealousy, and vengeance, towards God and Abel, had caused him to disgrace Mother Earth, Cain saw the future. He could feel the power of the Earth's wrath, such that Cain was humbled. He knew his sin had caused great pains and he was to be held responsible. Just as Adam and Eve (and the serpent) took their medicine, so too would Cain.

This admission can be seen in Cain addressing YAHWEH, admitting "My punishment" (" *ă·wō·nî*"). It also recognized his God was indeed "great," such that one word can translate as meaning much "greater than I." It is possible to have Cain say, "I can bear my punishment," or admit the "punishment for inequity" is indeed his justly "to carry." Still, the focus on "I," meaning one alone, without YAHWEH, without Mother Earth, without his mother and father's support, Cain stated his help will come from elsewhere.

If Cain had felt it would be impossible for him to bear the

Chapter 4: The initial punishment of Cain

punishment, as a murderer he would know how to kill a hero. He could have committed suicide or asked YAHWEH to end his life. However, the LORD was not punishing Cain for having killed his brother (the Earth was), so YAHWEH would have denied that request.

That means it makes much more sense to see the holy lineage of Cain being his only recourse. As coming from the loins of the Son of God, Cain knew he had a role to play, as a priest. YAHWEH had come to Cain and told him, "You have dominion over sin," but Cain chose to allow Satan to reign over him. Satan would then become Cain's ally in this punishment that he could not bear alone. Cain was accepting the punishment of the LORD, in the same way he accepted a life of evil. Cain's statement was one that said he would become the Father of a line of priests who would mislead the human beings of the earth, and continue to insult all gods who serve God and man.

---

14 *Behold, Thou hast driven me out this day from the face of the land; and from Thy face shall I be hid; and I shall be a fugitive and a wanderer in the earth; and it will come to pass, that whosoever findeth me will slay me.'*

די וְהֵ תָּשְׁרַג יִתָּא הָיוֹס, עֵמָעַל יִגַּף הָאָדָמָה, דִּינֶפָמוּ, רִתֵּסָאֶ; יִתִיָּיהָן עַנַ דְנַנ, אַרְאָבּ, הָיָחָן לְךָ-יִאָצְמ, יִנֶגְרְהַי.

D2 *See cast out the day upon face of earth face to hide to become to quiver to wander land to come to pass all to find to kill.*

Cain confirms his dedication to Satan, by telling YAHWEH

The Cain & Abel Story

to watch him hide from the face of the earth. In the story of the battle of Heaven, between the angels who obeyed God (to serve man) and those who rebelled (refusing to serve man), the fallen angels were cast into the pits of the earth. Cain says to the LORD now, "Use your all-seeing eye to see where I go." The statement, "From Thy face shall I be hid," means Cain will not face God. He will face Lucifer.

The word appearing in verse 12, *"nu-awh nud"* or *"nah haw-nud"* ("דנע ענ"), which is translated as "a fugitive and a wanderer," is repeated here. The same translation applies. However, it is one thing to be outcast and forced to forever wander the earth, but this verse now proclaims that Cain has been cast from the face of the land. The standard King James translation (above) states, "a wanderer in the earth," not "on the earth," although "on the earth" could be read.

When one reads *nu-awh nud* as "quiver to move to and fro," this then changes the "vagabond wanderer" into one who has to seek out safe shelter, in addition to needing to forage for food to stay alive. This makes the aspect of being hidden from the face mean not only the face of YAHWEH but the surface of the Earth. This means Cain was forced to seek a dwelling inside the earth, in the most solid and hard parts of the earth, which are caves.

When the element of Cain expressing fear is read into these words, one hears Cain lament about other people finding him and killing him. That way of reading this verse misses the primary point. Cain is, in essence, a convicted murderer who will spend the rest of his life living in caves and foraging for food. He will have to move from cave to cave in order to have a safe place to sleep and give the land's natural food sources time to produce its fruits and harvests. Still, since he cannot live on the face of the land, and because there would be winter months to contend with

Chapter 4: The initial punishment of Cain

when food will not be plentiful naturally, Cain will have to store what he finds.

This then leads one to see Cain dwelling in caves, where dried fruits and grains would be stored for future use. In that case, anyone who found one of Cain's stashes of food would be a danger to Cain. That would more often be animals, rather than humans; but it could also be people seeking shelter or hunting for animals. In order to protect his hard won possessions, and also to satisfy a taste for meat developed through the sacrifice of animals as a priest, Cain will most likely be the one killing any living creature that would find him. In the case of human life being taken again, that would be yet another level of sin to which Cain would fall.

As to the killing aspect of verse 14, it is important to jump ahead in the story of Genesis and remember that all of the Patriarchs up until the Great Flood, and including Noah, lived for time spans that are above and beyond the life spans of typical mortals. There can be no confusing the number of years each lived as being anything other than solar years, which were the same then as they are today. The great life spans must be attributed to the direct link to the Son of Man and his connection to immortality as a heavenly creation. This means all descendants of Adam are heroes, much like those portrayed in movies today.

This hero status means death does not come easily to them, as they have a level of heavenly protection assisting them. It may or may not be that Cain had significant physical strengths; but he would certainly be more naturally resistant to diseases, well beyond mere mortals. This means that a mere mortal would not stand a chance of killing Cain, should one attempt that, should Cain be caught taking food from someone's garden. While Cain could have strength comparable to someone like Hercules, it is more likely his strongest bodily feature was his brain.

The Cain & Abel Story

Cain was able to kill his hero brother because of his being assisted by the devil (according to other legends), so he had learned to be crafty and sly. Having killed once, and with a life sentence in tow, Cain clearly had nothing to lose, should he kill someone he deemed as a threat to him or his food supply.

This is why one should see verse 14 setting up the next verse. Cain was not moaning to YAHWEH about being cast out amid killers, seeking protection for himself. He knew he would be punished for hundreds of years, so his own death would shorten the sentence. Cain was threatening the LORD, telling God he had best protect all mortal people who may wander upon him, unknowingly. Remember, there were no books to let anyone know that Cain was the murderer of his brother, outcast by Mother Earth. There would be no one seeking him on purpose (like a bounty hunter), wanting to kill him.

---

15 *And the LORD said unto him: 'Therefore whosoever slayeth Cain, vengeance shall be taken on him sevenfold.' And the LORD set a sign for Cain, lest any finding him should smite him.*

ט וַיֹּאמֶר לוֹ יְהוָה לָכֵן כָּל־הֹרֵג קַיִן, שִׁבְעָתַיִם יֻקָּם; וַיָּשֶׂם יְהוָה לְקַיִן אוֹת, לְבִלְתִּי הַכּוֹת־אֹתוֹ כָּל־מֹצְאוֹ.

H2 *To say YHWH thus all to kill Cain seven times take vengeance. To set YHWH Cain a sign not to smite all to find.*

This verse continues the statement made in the previous verse, where YAHWEH addresses the issue raised by Cain, about "all to find to kill." It appears, and has been translated as such,

Chapter 4: The initial punishment of Cain

as if YAHWEH accepted Cain's argument that his fear will cause others to seek him out to kill him. For that reason of acceptance, the LORD decreed that anyone who finds and kills Cain will be punished sevenfold.

That argument is akin to trying to answer the question, "If a tree falls in the woods and no one is around, does it make a sound?" Who would know Cain murdered his brother? Who would think that Mother Earth had made life hard for Cain? No one but Adam and Eve knew that history, and they would not try to kill their own son.

Reading the verse as if Cain were trying to trick YAHWEH into easing the sentence by the Earth goddess would be reasonable. He can be seen doing that by seeming to admit his punishment is justified and he is willing to bear that responsibility. However, he then tells the LORD how accepting that punishment might make him murder again, in defense of his cave home and stored possessions.

This flaw, as well as Cain knowing YAHWEH knew everything, means verse 15 is stating, "Whoever Cain slays, vengeance will be taken upon him seven times." The vengeance would be a curse from anyone losing a loved one at the expense of Cain.

Because God knew the heart and mind of Cain (and everyone else he created), He sees through any potential of Cain's language being designed to deceive. The LORD knew the intent of what Cain said, so YAHWEH set judgment on Cain, in advance of him acting upon his threats. Instead of trying to convince the Earth Mother to ease her punishment, God tells Cain that if he kills anyone other than Abel, his punishment will be sevenfold. To add to that amendment, God tells Cain he is now to be marked so anyone who finds him will run, for fear of his own death.

This makes the "mark of Cain" or the "sign for Cain" be something quite visible, which would instantly cause mortals to flee. While this has been long thought to be some physical feature that many have tried to figure out (with no strong consensus or proof to support any and all theories), one must use the words of the story to get a grasp of what sign the LORD would use to make Cain identifiable to everyone who found him.

The element of the story that Cain identifies with, because of his lowered countenance, is evil. Evil had come previously in the form of the serpent, which God made to crawl upon the ground for its sin in Eden. God made the serpent as he made all the wild animals, and God made the serpent the craftiest of them all. Still, the serpent was a physical form that took pleasure in tricking the half-human-half-god children of Heaven without forcing them to do anything.

This means the serpent was an instrument of evil, which is under the influence of the god called Lucifer, the fallen angel. Cain willingly allowed this evil presence to have dominion over him, killing his brother and threatening God that he might kill others. Then, just as YAHWEH punished the serpent, Cain would be given a similar punishment. The serpent lost its legs to forever crawl in the dirt, away from the ears of humans. Likewise, Cain would be physically changed to warn the innocent to stay away from Cain.

In Hebrew, the word "*ha-satan*" ("וְטָשָׂה"), translated as Satan, means "the opposer." This title has been applied to one who is half-human-half-god and has been given other titles as well in biblical literature. For this reason, seeing how Cain was of blood half-human and half-god, I see the mark placed upon him to be one that has commonly been depicted in art over the millennia.

Chapter 4: The initial punishment of Cain

This means that Cain was to be "the opposer" of any mortals who would find him, thus identified as a monster that would strike fear in those who found him.

I see how this could easily be the addition of horns on his head, as art has depicted satyrs. Since he was to dwell in caves, most probably in mountainous regions of what is today western Iran, he might have a greyish color skin, with fur or thick hair on his body. Perhaps, he was given goat-like eyes, cloven feet, and even a pointed tail. Any of these features would be an instant sign for all to beware a creature that was in no way "humane." I believe Cain became the prototype for the Devil, but one which would ultimately die.

This makes the punishment of "seven times" important to understand. Cain has already been punished by the Earth Mother to a natural life of hard surface to dwell in. Cain tried to trick God into lessening that punishment by threatening to kill again. This makes YAHWEH place punishment upon Cain for having killed his brother, as not only one life span but seven. This then becomes the life span of Cain's descendants, which is why the story goes in that direction next. Cain was told by God that his one murder will take seven lifetimes to serve, without any more killing of human beings.

Chapter 5

The lineage of Cain

16 *And Cain went out from the presence of the LORD, and dwelt in the land of Nod, on the east of Eden.*

טז וַיֵּצֵא קַיִן, מִלִּפְנֵי יְהוָה; וַיֵּשֶׁב בְּאֶרֶץ-נוֹד, קִדְמַת-עֵדֶן.

V2 *To go out Cain face YHWH to dwell land Nod east Eden.*

The word "Nod" is a form of the word "*nud*," which was used in the punishment of Cain by Mother Earth. That word was used when YAHWEH told Cain he must be a "vagabond and wanderer." The word translated as "to wander" was "*nud*." Thus many see this "land of Nod" as representative of the place Cain would go to always move "to and fro." Still, when the word is seen as a statement about the land itself, then Nod would be a place that "quivers," "wanders," or "moves to and fro." That would be an indication that the "land of Nod" was a region prone to earth-

Chapter 5: The lineage of Cain

quakes, with rocky mountainous soil, where natural caves would be found.

When one believes that Eden represented a specific place on the earth, in the Fertile Crescent region between the Tigris and Euphrates Rivers, then Nod would be east of there. Prehistorically, those two rivers flowed to a much higher Persian Gulf, where its shorelines made the city of Ur a port location and the two rivers did not join in a delta region. Ur was on the banks of the Euphrates River; and, it should be recalled, Ur was where Abraham lived, before being told by YAHWEH to leave.

If one sees how Abraham was descended from Adam, and from Noah, then it would make sense that Noah and Lamech would travel from Mount Ararat (where the Ark landed) back to their homeland. If Ur was the place of Adam, between the Euphrates and Tigris rivers, that fits Adam's banishment from Eden, to "east of Eden." The waters of that gulf have receded, such that the ruins of Ur are now over 100 miles inland. This means Adam would have toiled within the garden watered by two major rivers, east of Ur.

Since Adam and Eve were in a heavenly place called Eden, it was not a true earthly environment. I believe the point on the Earth that links to Heaven is where Jerusalem is today. That ancient city was called Salem, with Melchizedek the King and priest over that place. He was known for his immortality, having never been born or died. Melchizedek reigned over Salem, preceding the Great Flood, such that he was supposedly placed in the Garden of Eden (Heaven) while the flood waters covered the earth.

Melchizedek is said to have presented Abram with the robes of Adam during their meeting, according to the Second Book of Enoch. Thus, when one sees Salem as the portal to the spiritual

The Cain & Abel Story

realm, then that would be where Adam exited Heaven. With cherubim guarding Salem behind him, Adam would then have gone east, to the Euphrates River, where Ur would later be founded by Adam's descendants.

Cain was then banished further to the east of Eden, beyond the Tigris River. There, the land is less fertile and rocky. One would not have to travel far "east of Eden," if this were indeed the location, to reach the Zagros Mountains, which form the border between modern Iraq and Iran. That region is where one of the oldest cities has been unearthed, named Sosa (Iran). This could be where we are instructed to find Cain.

The Zagros Mountains were geologically formed by the movement of the Arabian tectonic plate against the Eurasian plate (or Iranian plate). This movement can then be seen as the "land of Wandering," such that there are now 3 centimeters of movement each year. In much older times, it may be the movement was greater. The Zagros Mountains are referred to as "folded mountains," meaning the ends of the mountain range are pushed together, causing the middle region to fold and ripple. This means there are peaks and valleys that appear in a "zig zag" manner, and "zig zag" being another way of saying "to and fro." That could be the operative translation of "*nud*."

The geology of this region is mostly limestone and dolomite based rock formations, with mudstone and siltstone having eroded there over the ages. Erosion has formed the ridges. Due to the formation of salt domes and glaciers, petroleum has been trapped under this mountain range. Iran's largest oil fields are found in the plateau just to the east of the Zagros range.

The ecology is forest and forest steppe, which is known for trees that produce nuts, like pistachios and almonds. In ancient times, there is evidence the region naturally produced grasses

Chapter 5: The lineage of Cain

with grains, like wheat and barley. Some of the earliest dated evidence of wine storage comes from archeological finds in this region. Wild grapes could then be another of the fruits Cain found growing naturally in Nod, making it an appealing place to settle.

---

17 *And Cain knew his wife; and she conceived, and bore Enoch; and he built a city, and called the name of the city after the name of his son Enoch.*

יי עֲדֵיֵו וְיִק תֵא-תִשָּׂאוּ, רַחֵתֵן דְּלָתֵּי תֵא-חֵנוֹךְ; יְהִיֵ, רִיעַ הֹנֵב, סֵס אָרְקִיֵו
רִיעָה, סְשֵׁךְ וֹנבּ חֵנוֹךָ.

22 *To know Cain woman to conceive to beget Enoch to come to pass to build excitement [city] to proclaim to name excitement [city] a name son Enoch.*

Here we find evidence that Adam and Eve were not the first human beings on planet earth, simply because Cain has found a wife. If Adam and Eve are believed to be the first humans God created, then faith in the Holy Bible begins to crumble when the first elementary school student asks, "Where did Cain's wife come from?" The only female available, according to that misinterpretation, was Eve; but Cain did not sleep with his mother.

As stated previously, man and women were created on the sixth day. Ages of human males and females evolved around the planet, migrating through all the continents. That was established well before God rested on the seventh day, which He "blessed" and "consecrated," as a holy period called a "day."

The Cain & Abel Story

That was when God created His Son (and daughter) who would become the first priest to YAHWEH. Adam and Eve were sent to an already established world where mankind existed.

This means Cain took a woman from the general population. A normal human female would not be expected to have a life span beyond what was normal during that age of time. This would mean the interbreeding of God-made heroes with normal human beings for the purpose of creating priests would begin with Cain. The descendants of Adam, including Cain and Seth, would take normal human females for wives. This would have no effect on the life spans of the earliest children born of such holy blood; but those first wives, from general stock, would not have lived to see their husbands' deaths. Eventually, a bloodline of princes and princesses would spread, with both sexes carrying this longevity trait. However, as time would pass, the royal bloodline would find less and less longevity of life, until interbreeding would largely eliminate this observable link to an immortal beginning.

This is a good place to interject the use of the word "*'iš·tōw*" ("אִשְׁתּוֹ"), which is translated as "wife." The word is rooted in "*ishshah*" ("נָשִׁים"), which can mean "wife, female, or woman." The intent is to show someone of the opposite sex, because the purpose for "knowing" her was to make a child. Thus, a "wife" is one whom a "husband" impregnates for the purpose of begetting offspring. Because Cain had been banished from his place with Adam and Eve, there was no ceremony that determined that a "female" or a "woman" was a "wife." A "woman" was a "wife" because she became with child, and no other reason.

Cain's wife bore him a son, who Cain named Enoch. At this point, the names that commence become the only way to grasp the reasons why Cain's lineage is introduced. In all of the Old

Chapter 5: The lineage of Cain

Testament, the names play the same role of importance, as the Hebrew people who wrote the books of the Holy Bible used meaningful words as names. There never was an instance where one of the Patriarchs of the children of God named a child simply because they liked the name, or it sounded nice. Names were a statement about the child; and we know the statement Cain made with the birth of his son by knowing the meaning of "Enoch."

According to abarim-publications.com, and their page on the etymology and meaning of biblical names, they state:

> "The name Enoch comes from the verb חָנַךְ (*hanak*) meaning dedicate, begin. HAW Theological Wordbook of the Old Testament notes, "With one exception (Proverbs 22:6), hanak and its derivates refer to an action in connection to a building (1 Kings 8:63), wall (Nehemiah 12:27), an altar (Numbers 7:10), or an image (Daniel 3:2)."

They then list another source lexicon that states the word "*hanak*" also has Chaldean meaning, relative to: "imprint, pierce into, instruct, make wise." This leads to the derivative "*hanik*," which means, "trained servant."

When one sees Enoch being named as a "trained servant of the altar" or a "trained servant of a building," one can then connect this to Cain having been born to become a priest. All of the lineage of Adam would be born believers in religion, with one of the Generations of Adam being named Enoch, the son of Jared, the great grandfather of Noah. However, because Cain had chosen to become a priest "to oppose" YAHWEH, by offering his sacrifices to Lucifer, his fallen angel-god, Enoch would follow along this line.

This then explains that Cain would become the first priest serving Satan (by whatever name fits best: Devil-Lucifer-Bee-

The Cain & Abel Story

lzebub, et al names of evil personified). Enoch, Cain's first-born male son, was dedicated to serve the crafty serpent's influencer also. He would be a trained servant to a lesser god.

When one sees Cain fulfilling his mission to be a priest, only as the initiator of an evil cult one can then see the word "*iyr*" ("עיר") differently. That word is regularly read as meaning "city," but the word primarily means "excitement." This means that Cain and Enoch built a "stirring" and "activity." This is then another way of saying "quivering to and fro," which is the word written that projected Cain as a wanderer. While that action and movement are also descriptive of the hustle and bustle that characterizes an area where many people live, it is more likely that such attraction would be required first, before one could build a city.

Since the population, at first, was only Cain, his woman and son Enoch, to build a city means people have to be attracted. Otherwise there is no need for nor enough inhabitants to deem a place as being a city. The word "build" would require much effort gathering the necessary materials to physically erect buildings, of which a city had many. It is much easier to build excitement, because that is as little as lighting a fire and making some noise. In those ancient times, excitement would have been like a light in the night to moths, enticing people to come live where the action is.

Keep in mind that Cain was probably a cave dweller, a hunter-gatherer, and one who used his cunning more than his brawn. A city implies many people living in close proximity to one another; but one must remember that God placed a mark on Cain, so others would recognize the danger he represented. When human beings saw Cain, they would have been more likely to run away, than to ask him if he needed help building a

Chapter 5: The lineage of Cain

city. That mark certainly would hinder that endeavor. However, Cain's son, Enoch, might not have been so marked.

Enoch was the one whose name dedicated him as a trained servant. With Cain's help (and the woman as well), Enoch could have created activity, while also erecting an altar for sacrifices. The human beings that lived in Nod, or migrated through there, could be attracted to the altar and the ritual ceremonies performed on it. The humans would not be familiar with what a priest was, or who he served. Adam fell to earth to bring the awareness of sin to those who knew nothing of good or bad. Cain, on the other hand, was dedicated to Satan, so Enoch would be trained to serve evil as a priest. Therefore, Cain and Enoch would build the first temple to a god, only it would not honor YAHWEH.

When it is written, "to proclaim to name excitement" or "to call to name city" ("*way-yiq-rah shem ha-ir*" – "וִיקְרָא שֵׁם הָעִיר"), this is not so much announcing the name of a place, but a call to people to serve a deity. It becomes a statement that Enoch was dressed in priestly robes, causing the excitement of a pagan ritual, attracting pilgrims who heard all the hubbub. All of this would have taken place while Cain stayed hidden in his cave, not to be seen.

The probability of animal sacrifice would send out the smell of cooking meat that would attract humans from long distances. Cain, based on the mythology of other versions of the Cain and Abel story, knew how to kill with a blade. He would have trained Enoch in the skill of flint knife use. They could have trapped animals and offered them "to the gods," as a way of attracting customers with goods to trade. Over time, the facility built by Cain and Enoch would have increased, due to extra helping hands, so that it would have been known as a place to visit, if

The Cain & Abel Story

not pilgrimage to for the first religious purposes. If enough people plan to be present frequently enough, a city would have been the result, with Cain and Enoch having to do little of the work.

It may also be that the excitement was in the sharing of priestly duties. That would mean the altar of Cain and Enoch became the place where trained servants or prepared ministers of rites were sent out into the world. The more people that were attracted to that place over and over again, as returning pilgrims would create a need for new members serving the world's first religion. Those would have been initiated and dedicated to serve in a temple of sorts. Understanding such early roots of religion stemming from Cain teaching humans about many gods of power means one can understand when the Holy Bible turns its focus towards all the people who served Ba'als, their beginnings would stem from the "place named after Enoch."

---

18 *And unto Enoch was born Irad; and Irad begot Mehujael; and Mehujael begot Methushael; and Methushael begot Lamech.*

חי דְּלֵנִיּוּ ,דְּונחַל ,דְרִיעָן-תאֶ ,דְרִיעָן; לאֱיָּוחמְ-תאֶ דְלַי ,לאֱיָּחמְוּ ,דְלַי תאֶ-
דְּמֶלָ-תאֶ דְלַי ,לאֱשָׁוּתמְוּ ,לאֱשָׁוּתמְ.

Ch2 *To beget Enoch Irad Irad beget Mehujael Mehujael beget Methusael Methusael beget Lamech.*

In this one verse we see a rapid progression of descendants in the lineage of Cain. Other than four more children of Cain's blood being born, it can appear to become a relatively meaningless statement. As it is with all lengthy verses and chapters in the

Chapter 5: The lineage of Cain

Old Testament that state one begat after another, this verse passes before a reader's eyes like, "blah, blah, blah, blah," That is, unless one translates the names into important words of meaning.

Enoch had Cain's grandson, meaning he too had found a wife, but in this verse the wives are of no importance to mention. Enoch chose the name "Irad" for his son, which is similar to the Hebrew word "*yarad*" ("יָרַד") which means "go down, descend, decline." An additional letter brings about the word "*ya-ir*" ("רִיעַ"), which returns a focus to "excitement," the root word linking Cain and Enoch to a "city."

This means the birth of Irad meant the activity of the altar took a downward direction, which was further away from YAHWEH, more in the direction of evil. Keep in mind how a lowered countenance had Cain laying on the ground, opening the gateway for evil to have dominion over him. By naming a priest Irad, Enoch intended a form of worship that created more "excitement," increasing the reach of a "city." His training of Irad would then be to attract worshippers who would put themselves in that lowered position, where evil could take control over them.

From Irad comes a son given the name Mehuja-el. This name combines two words, where many names of the Hebrews include "*el*" ("אֵל") in them, meaning "God." The reason is their child being named as a dedication to "God." In this name we find dedication is not the intent, as "*macha*" ("יִמְחֶה") means "to wipe out" or "to strike." Thus, Irad named his son as a dedication "to erase God" from the list of "gods," or "*elohim*," whom priests served.

The name Mehuja-el is then a name with a dual meaning. The great grandson of Cain was dedicated to the destruction of knowledge of YAHWEH, as One God to fear; but he was also dedicated to the one god who wipes out those who come under

83

The Cain & Abel Story

his influence (Satan). This descendant of Cain played the role of celebrant to all who would be "Destroyed of God."

From the great grandson of Cain came another son. Mehuja-el named him Methusa-el, which is another combination of words, with "God" being the final focus. In this case, "Methusa" is a series of words (a sentence) that breaks down into "*Mat-oo-sha*," which means either, "Who wars directly with" or "Who dies straight of." The link to "*el*" is then both a designation away from the One God, as an indicator of a lesser god who rules over war and death.

The combination of phonetics that produce "*she'el*" at the end is then a link to the sound of "*she'ol*," the Hebrew word meaning "hell." As such, this son of Mehuja-el is not a turn back towards favor of YAHWEH (as some scholars seem ready to believe). Instead, this name represents a further descent way from the LORD. This name introduces a son who would become a priest who dedicated corpses to the lowest depths of hell, as servants of Lucifer.

From Methusa-el came the last name in verse 18, Lamech. There is some difference of opinion as to the roots and particles that can attach to this name's meaning. According to the website abarim-publications.com, and their page on the etymology of biblical names, one source that site refers to is reported to state:

> "The name Lamech may also be seen as constructed of the particle (*le*), meaning to or towards; and the verb דוּמ (*muk*), be low, depressed, or even the adjacent verb דָּכָ (*makak*), be low, humiliated. The whole name would thus mean For Lowering; For Humiliation."

This contrasts with another source that debates the name as either meaning "Wild Man" or "Powerful." When all is com-

Chapter 5: The lineage of Cain

bined, then one can come to a fuller understanding of this descendant of Cain. We can see how Methusa-el named Lamech in dedication to being a lower level priest, one who would initiate worship to his god through acts of humiliation.

Again, the act of lowering is in line with Cain having been in a lowered state, where he willingly allowed himself to be easily influenced by evil. Humiliation becomes a purposeful debasing of one's self, as an insult to YAHWEH. It represents a dedication of one more of Cain's line to Satan, for the promise of earthly delights and pleasures.

When verse 18 is read as a whole statement where the names blend into an important series of developments being explained, the list of five names (Enoch to Lamech) is then relative to the sevenfold punishment of Cain. When Cain is seen as the first, then Lamech represents the sixth generation of Cain. We are prepared for one more line to be born.

Still, when the meanings of the names are substituted, a much deeper statement appears. This too is relative to the sevenfold punishment of Cain. As such, the verse can read as follows:

> "And was born altar dedication [Enoch] to excite downward [Irad]. To declining excitement [Irad] was born the erasure of YAHWEH [Mehuja-el]. The the destroyer through a lesser god [Mehuja-el] was born death to hell [Methusael]. To this combat against YAHWEH [Methusa-el] was born for humiliation [Lamech]."

When this verse is read with the meanings shown, one comes away with a clear idea of Cain's punishment. He would be responsible for bringing about sons who would follow in his footsteps of stubborn self-righteousness. Because Cain was not willing to listen to YAHWEH and learn humility, his ego and de-

The Cain & Abel Story

sire to be godlike would become his own punishment. He would completely humiliate and lower his own name.

Still, the story is not yet completed. When counting from Cain (1), to Enoch (2), to Irad (3), to Mehujael (4), to Methusael (5), to Lamech (6), there is still one generation of lives remaining before Cain's punishment for murder would be completely served. The names of that generation are next.

---

19 *And Lamech took unto him two wives; the name of one was Adah, and the name of the other Zillah.*

ט **יט** וַיִּקַּח־לוֹ לֶמֶךְ, שְׁתֵּי נָשִׁים: שֵׁם הָאַחַת עָדָה, וְשֵׁם הַשֵּׁנִית צִלָּה.

T2 *To take Lamech two wife the name one Adah the name second Zillah.*

This verse begins by stating that Lamech "took to him two wives," where the verb "*way-yiq-qua*" ("וַיִּקַּח") begins this statement. The root word of "*way-yiq-qua*" is "*laquach*," which means Lamech could have "bought, captured, accepted, obtained, procured, seized, selected, took away, used," or even "married" two females. This is stated differently than verse 17, where it says "Cain knew his wife" ("*way-ye-dah*," root "*yada*," meaning "to know"). The same verb ("*way-ye-dah*") is chosen for Adam knowing Eve, in verse 4:1, so the use of "*laquach*" ("*law-kakh*") is significant.

The verb infinitive, "to take," implies something less than a natural attraction brought Lamech and his wives together. When two human beings of the opposite sex encounter one another

Chapter 5: The lineage of Cain

for the first time, there is the establishment of an emotional connection. Normal relationships are where both parties enjoy the presence of each other and want to remain together. When this relationship reaches the point where the two lay together in sexual intercourse, the element of "knowing" gives the connotation of intimacy.

To call this exchange an act of taking then lowers it to an animal level, as if Lamech had proven himself to be the alpha male. His position of strength would then have made him the rightful owner of the females, with it his duty to impregnate them. The implication is the "taking" was without any emotion present, other than lust. This one verb's use is then indicative of love being removed from this exchange.

In this verse we also have the first instance where one of the children of Adam had more than one wife. This also cannot be overlooked or seen as a normal circumstance for a priestly male. Even though there are stories of one man having sex with more than one woman (Abraham, Jacob, and David, as examples), and some having multiple wives where love initiated the relationships (David, more so than the others), the element of bigamy is introduced under suspect circumstances. Thus, one should not read having multiple wives as a standard allowed to some.

Since there was no formal rite of marriage at that early stage of mankind, beyond the production of live-born progeny, having multiple wives can be seen as Lamech seeking the blessing of two gods. Because he was one in a line of priests, the symbolism (as stated by Jesus much later) is he represents the bridegroom in a metaphoric marriage. The bride then represents the church, through which the bridegroom serves his master, a god or God. Multiple wives then allows for multiple churches to be the purpose, so that Lamech was ceremoniously serving different gods

The Cain & Abel Story

at one time.

Because we are deep into the lineage of Cain with Lamech, and because Cain's legacy is one of disrepute, I believe it is better to assume Lamech's taking of two wives is a first for pagan worshipers. I do not feel that Lamech cared for his wives before having sex with them, such that "taking two wives" is close to the practice of arranged marriage. That would imply some bargaining took place beforehand. I see the root emotion as being more in line with lust and rape, which would be as a ceremonial duty of the priest Lamech grew to become, Each marriage symbolized the dedication of Lamech to multiple deities. I got this feeling before understanding the names of his two wives; but that will further explain their relationship with Lamech.

The first wife taken by Lamech is Adah. According to abarim-publications.com, the word "*ada*" ("אָדָה") "is quite common," and they state "there is no way to know which of the many meanings" can be determined to be the true intent behind the name. For this reason, I believe it is important to realize all of the meanings, because Holy Scripture is sourced from God, and God does not speak in linear [only one meaning] ways. Their website states the word "אָדָה" bears these uses:

> "1) The Hebrew verb אָדָה (*ada*) means go on, pass by. Derivatives are continuing future, booty, prey, as far as, until, while.
>
> 2) The Hebrew verb אָדָה (*ada*) means to ornament, deck oneself. The derivative אֲדָה (*ada*) means ornaments.
>
> 3) The Hebrew verb יָעַד (*ya'ad*) means appoint, betroth, assemble, meet. The derivative עֵדָה (*eda*) means congregation.
>
> 4) The Hebrew verb דוּא ('*ud*) means return,

Chapter 5: The lineage of Cain

repeat. Derivations דֵעָה (*eda*) mean witness, testimony/ ies.
5) The Hebrew noun עִדָּה (*idda*) means menstruation."

Knowing that these possibilities of meaning are common, look and see if you can place all of them together into one statement that fits the scenario of Cain's lineage of priests serving evil. There is the element of passing on the lineage to the seventh generation of punishment ("go on, pass by, continuing future"). The woman taken, called Adah, is "booty" and/or "prey," more than she is someone known on a personal and emotional depth. When Adah is taken, she is dressed "ornately," as if in a ceremonial rite. She is presented not in a private chamber, but instead before a "congregation, assembly" or "meeting" of "witnesses." Finally, this woman called Adah is presented after she has begun her monthly cycle. This last point is important to understand fully.

The Israelites, who would become God's chosen people, to become His priests, were given specific instructions as to how menstruating women should be treated. They were to be kept in special tents until their flow had ceased. There was a period of eight days that a woman was deemed impure after any spillage of bodily fluids. That included blood and embryonic fluids from childbirth, meaning they were deemed impure during all monthly menstrual periods.

This impurity meant menstruating women had to be segregated, so they would not come into contact with anything deemed holy. That specifically meant they had to remain out of the Temple. Mary's purification rite at the Temple, with the baby Jesus, is an excellent example of how an impure woman was seen during times of bodily discharges, and how purification

The Cain & Abel Story

was required. Even as the Virgin Mother of Christ, Mary knew she must maintain the rites of purification and stay away from anything holy until predetermined time periods had passed.

When this is understood, one can then see how a ceremonial rite where a priest forcibly took an impure woman in front of a gathering of "church" members would be an insult to YAHWEH. One could presume the sex act was performed on the altar, where bodily fluids would be captured for burning. Thus, the name Adah makes a huge statement about Lamech and those followers of the god to whom Lamech would then be married.

It shows how a common woman (*ada* being a common word) was "taken" for this purpose. She would be presented in the temple of Lamech when her time of the month would be known to come. The timing of her cycle would have determined when a public ritual would be planned, as a ritual performance. It shows a very evil side of Lamech and shows how impure this religion would become.

The second (or "other") wife taken by Lamech was then named Zillah. The word "*tsil-law*" ("הִלָּצְ") is said to have four possible meanings, again by the website of Biblical name meanings and lexicons - abarim-publications.com. They say word group comes from "not very positive" roots. The four meanings are:

> "1) לָלַל (*salal*), means to tingle or quiver. The derivatives of this root cover a whirring or buzzing and things that whirr: לְצַלְצ (*silsal*), meaning spear, locusts, and things that ring: (bells, cymbals).
> 2) לָלַל (*salal* II), means to sink or submerge (Exodus 15:10 only).
> 3) לָלַל (*salal* III) means to be or grow dark

Chapter 5: The lineage of Cain

(Nehemiah 3:19). Derivative צל (*sel*) means shadow. The female form of this word would yield the name Zillah.

4) צָלַל (*sll* IV) is the assumed root of צלול (*slwl*); the killer cake of Judges 7:13."

Again, when one sees the words of God as not being limited in meaning, thereby Zillah was a name chosen with all possible meaning intended, the second wife of Lamech can also be seen as a woman taken, just as was Adah. In the case of Zillah, she can be understood as an intended to introduce a certain "tingle" of excitement [remember the word meaning "city" also means "excitement"] to Lamech's second church. As part of Zillah's adornments, she could be wearing bells or have cymbals on her fingers. This could be seen as an indication of the first use of dance in a ceremonial rite, as finger cymbals are believed to be part of the earliest forms of dance.

The possibility of Zillah being submerged or sinking, this can be seen as a further lowering of religious ritual to depths never before reached. It could also be an indication of a sexual act being performed underwater, which would be a perverted foreshadowing of baptism with water, where water and religious ritual have been merged. Keep in mind that "water" is an element of the physical realm, one that is symbolic of human changing emotional states. It can be an element that cleanses and refreshes, while also being one that excites and pleases.

The aspect of "shadow" and "darkness" can be found supporting a theme of devil worship, which is the opposite of the religion that would be led by YAHWEH. Jesus is the light, where light and the sun are the symbols of the guidance of the LORD, which keeps one from stumbling and falling. However, this element of Zillah's name could also indicate that she had a

The Cain & Abel Story

dark complexion, representing the first inter-racial marriage, as an offering to those worshippers of a darker-colored skin.

Finally, the "killer cake" of Judges 7:13 is explained as a "round loaf of barley bread," one which rolled down a hill and collapsed a tent. A "round loaf" indicates bread with yeast; and as a "cake" it is a sweet bread, rather than basic flatbread. This can then indicate some form of bread being passed around, perhaps with each participant dipping that risen bread into an impure blood.

Again, bread foreshadows the body of Christ, meaning the physical manifestations of the earthly realm that projected his coming. The unleavened bread of the Passover is thus without embellishment, requiring the Holy Spirit for understanding. A symbolic cake from Zillah would be clearly stating its meaning, such that consumption would bind one to a god that killed one's soul.

In all cases, as suggested by the website of biblical name meanings, Zillah would be a name that introduces unfavorable practices into religion. It must then be noticed that both of the wives taken by Lamech do not necessarily become impregnated during the ceremonial event; but since Lamech came from hero blood, one must assume he had a powerful impact upon the women with whom he had sex. The implication is the children these women produced came to him from sex during ritual acts. These would have been conceived without any form of emotional love and purely for the purpose of bringing more shame upon the name of Cain.

---

20 *And Adah bore Jabal; he was the father of such as dwell in tents and have cattle.*

Chapter 5: The lineage of Cain

‎כ הַנֹּקְמוּ לְהֵא בַּשִׁי, יִבָּא--הָיָה אוּה ׃לְבָנָי-תֵא, הֹדָעַ דְּלֶתֵּו.

Y2 *Beget Adah Jabal he come to pass father to dwell a tent cattle.*

When the name Adah is simplified to bear the one meaning "Ornament" (as summed up by abarim-publications.com), we see that from that "source of pride, honor, or credit" (a definition of "ornament") was born Jabal, a son. The name Jabal means, "bring, carry, lead," or "conduct," coming from the root "*yabal*" ("לבַיָ"). That word, as found in Isaiah, can also mean "watercourse," with "*yubal*" ("לבַוּיִ") meaning "stream." When read as "*yobel*" (also "לבֵוֹיִ"), a meaning of "trumpet" comes.

Because one is then told that Jabal will become a father, the meaning is that Jabal will become the first of a kind of people. He can be seen as the "leader" his name implies. Still, he symbolizes the first who will "carry" the religion established in Nod, in the place called Enoch, to other parts of the earth (relative to that vicinity of the world) taking religion to the people as a missionary.

In order to travel as a priest, he would need to "carry" supplies with him. Jabal might best do that by following "water courses," going by raft along the shoreline. Rather than having to carry water, as well as portable altars and ritual sacrifice materials and supplies, a river would supply needed water. While travelling, Jabal would live in tents, or some portable shelter. However, one would not think the invention of the tent would come this late in the development of the world.

One has already read that the Earth Mother sentenced Cain to a life of wandering and being a vagabond. Discovering how

The Cain & Abel Story

that meant he would seek caves for shelter comes from reading between the lines, but one would first think a wanderer and vagabond would be the same as a nomad. While caves would be an instant place of shelter, the need to migrate to where food was plentiful would make portable shelter a necessary development to avoid the elements of heat and rain.

It is logical to assume clothing manufacture techniques would have already developed outside coverings, from sewing animal hides together creating tent dwellings. That would have been a natural need by Cain and Enoch, for builders to have cover during the erection of the "city" called Enoch. This means Jabal would not have been the first to travel with a tent; meaning the original element in verse 20 is found in the placement of "cattle" with tents.

Because Abel was a keeper of flocks (or herds), such that he watched over small cattle and/or sheep; the stated and implied meaning comes with the word "*tson*" ("וְאָצ"), in Genesis 4:2. Therefore, as grazing animals need to be moved from pasture to pasture so not to deplete their food source, a migrant rancher is a form of nomad facing the same problems with the physical elements. This means tents would have already been invented long before Jabal. Therefore, another way to read "the father to dwell a tent livestock" ("הַנְקָמוּ לְהָא בְשִׁי, יִבָאְ") makes more sense.

This interpretation requires that one again place focus on the lineage of Cain being priests to lesser gods, primarily those gods of evil and the angel Lucifer. This means Jabal is the first to take animal sacrifice on the road, with bulls being the specific sacrificial beast of choice [the "sacred bull"]. Jabal would then set out in a caravan that would represent the first "tent revival meeting tour." A bull's horn could be used as a "trumpet" to summon a crowd and announce that a ritual service for the people was there

Chapter 5: The lineage of Cain

for them. The element of a bull being sacrificed, with a burnt offering feast following, would undoubtedly draw a crowd. This can be seen as the first use of a horn in religious rites representing the precursor of the Hebrew *shofar* (from a ram's horn).

This statement of "cattle" being fathered, where the religious use of "father" should also be read into the meaning, is relative to the astrological ages of man. Those ages move from one astrological sign to the next, roughly over 2,000 to 2,500 years, based on a new North Star overhead. We are now in the beginning times of the Age of Aquarius (the Age of Mind or Knowledge). Prior to that was the Age of Pisces or the Fish (aligning with the Age of Jesus). That was preceded by the Age of Aries or the Ram (The Age of the One God). That was preceded by the Age of Taurus, or the Age of the Bull. That age was when people were taught to construct images and idols of bulls for the purpose of worship and dedication.

Once the Age of the Ram began, the children of Israel were being led to Mount Sinai where the presence of the LORD was announced with a *shofar*, from a cloud. When the fear of the people led them to think Moses had been killed, they reverted to past religious beliefs and constructed the golden calf idol. That has relevance in understanding how Jabal fathered the Age of the Bull by travelling to take ritual sacrifice to the people, along with worship to lesser deities.

Interestingly, the age of man that preceded the Age of Taurus was the Age of Gemini or the Age of the Twins. This would represent a time beginning when Cain and Abel were born, as I have theorized, as twins. Following the same logic, I see that Jabal was the first of two twin sons born to Lamech, through Adah. Lamech's second wife, Zillah, would also bear Lamech twins, one son and one daughter, although it is not expressly stated as

The Cain & Abel Story

"twins."

In both the Koran and Palestinian mythologies of the Cain and Abel story, Cain and Abel are described as each being a twin to a sister (not to each other), with the sisters to become each other's wives. While I do not see that as relevant to the story of Cain, it does show there has been some thought about twin births in Genesis 4. Regardless of the theories and mythologies, by seeing twin births early in the Book of Genesis one can see the Age of Gemini being fulfilled through the lineage of both Cain and Abel, where Abel is seen to be the soul reincarnated within Seth.

---

21 *And his brother's name was Jubal; he was the father of all such as handle the harp and pipe.*

כא וְשֵׁם אָחִיו, יוּבָל: הוּא הָיָה--אֲבִי, כָּל-תֹּפֵשׂ כִּנּוֹר וְעוּגָב.

A3 *A name brother Jubal he become father all to take hold of a lyre [stringed instrument] pipe [flute-like reed instrument].*

In reference to the twin theory, verse 23 again presents the birth of an offspring without any reference to a separate act of procreation. This is just as was with Adam and Eve, when Cain and Abel were born. As common as twin births are, and considering the evidence that fraternal twins can be genetically passed from generation to generation, I believe Jabal and Jubal are twins developed from two eggs released at the same time (fraternal twins). This would mean each child could be completely different in appearance, as was the case with Esau and Jacob. The

Chapter 5: The lineage of Cain

birth of twins would mean a second sexual encounter would not be necessary and that would support the concept of Lamech taking, rather than knowing his wives.

Regardless, the brother of Jabal is Jubal, which is a similar name bearing similar meaning, since Hebrew is a language of consonants with most vowels implied. As such, the abarim-publications.com website shows the meaning of Jabal and Jubal together [along with Tubal and Tubal-Cain]. They see the same meaning of "stream" as applying to Jubal, but not the meaning of "trumpet." They say that all of the names of Lamech's three male children are like "hour, minutes, and seconds, where their meaning cannot be assessed separately." As such, they conclude that Jubal is a name that refers to "Playing," with one source saying, "Joyful Sound, Music, and Jubilee." In the case of the latter, the word jubilee is associated with Jubal.

This name's meaning shows how Jubal would accompany his brother on their journeys, with both being missionaries. Their tent revival meetings would not only be announced with a horn blast highlighting an animal sacrifice and barbecue, but there was music provided to put the attendees in the mood. While their mother, Adah, introduced dance with finger cymbals, this means Jubal introduced the world to music as part of a religious ceremony. As the father of both the lyre (stringed instruments) and pipe (flute-like instruments with reeds), Jubal did not necessarily invent the instruments; but, instead, he incorporated their use for religious purposes.

This association of Jubal to the harp and pipe brings to mind the image of the Greek god Pan. Although Pan was the god of rustic music, his command of the pipes was enchanting. The god who perfected the lyre was Apollo, the sun god. Pan once challenged Apollo to a contest that Apollo won, but not without

The Cain & Abel Story

some merit given to Pan. Still, the image of Pan, who had the lower anatomy of a goat, including cloven feet (as a faun or satyr), makes one recall the possibility of the mark of Cain being similar physical attributes. The DNA of Cain would have been passed down through all generations, with Jubal being the first to display his ancestral animal characteristics. Perhaps a robe and hood concealed them?

There are several places in the Old Testament (Psalms and Isaiah, for two) that tell of singing and dancing while accompanied by "lyre and pipe" or "harp and flute." Isaiah references a group of people who pretend to be holding religious rites with this practice, but he points out they do not honor YAHWEH (Isaiah 5:12). This means that people are easily attracted to sounds such as horn blasts and music, which is the "excitement" of Enoch. The offspring of Lamech would spread that excitement beyond any "city" that may have been built by Cain, through the use of music. While music can elevate the spirits to a point of reverence, one must be careful not to worship the sound and forget the true purpose of a religious rite.

---

22 *And Zillah, she also bore Tubal-cain, the forger of every cutting instrument of brass and iron; and the sister of Tubal-cain was Naamah.*

כב וְצִלָּה גַם-הִוא, יָלְדָה אֶת-תּוּבַל קַיִן--לֹטֵשׁ, כָּל-חֹרֵשׁ נְחֹשֶׁת וּבַרְזֶל; וַאֲחוֹת תּוּבַל-קַיִן, נַעֲמָה.

B3 *Zillah also she beget Tubal-cain to sharpen all craftsmen bronze iron sister Tubal-cain Naamah.*

Chapter 5: The lineage of Cain

The use of "also," following the name Zillah, means she too gave birth to twins. Because verse 22 tells of two births, one son and one daughter, the "also" reference confirms that Adah delivered twins. It also can support the birth of fraternal twins, where a child of each sex is born to different eggs; but identical twins can also be indicated (in both sets).

The statement of Zillah's name, again, brings out how noises surrounded her (buzzing and ringing), and that she may have had dark skin. This could be part of why her twins are associated with brass and iron. The element of her name that can translate as sunken or submerged can be an indication of where metals were found (in places where water had exposed them from erosion), as well as the tempering aspect of cooling metals in water. The aspect of dark may play a role in why iron workers are called "blacksmiths," as the etymology has iron called a "black metal."

This aspect of "forging," which is what smiths and blacksmiths do, referring to the use of furnaces and hammers, is then associated with the son Tubal-cain. The word "Tubal" is said to mean, "Flowing Forth," which comes from the same verb forms that Jubal is believed to derive from. This means there are some who see it as a form of "*tebel*," meaning "World." I lean towards a more unique name meaning, especially since Tubal is linked to the word "*cain*."

Many seem to see "*cain*" as indicative of this being a descendant of Cain, which is true (he is a descendant), but it overlooks how Cain's name had meaning ("spear, stake, reed, stalk, acquire," etc.). Thus, the addition of "*cain*" to this child's name has less to do with an honor to Cain, and more to do with the meaning of that name. When one sees how Tubal-cain was to be

The Cain & Abel Story

a forger or craftsman of cutting or sharp edges made of brass and iron, when those instruments are added to the end of a "spear, shaft, stake," so that pole "acquired" a blade, the "World-spear" would become a military invention of great magnitude.

I actually see how Tubal-cain could have specialized in the fabrication of bronze spearheads and swords, while his sister was the one who worked with iron. While there is nothing said about the sister, other than her name,"Naamah," the word meaning "iron" ("לְבַרְזֶל" – "*u-bar-zel*") links to the word meaning "sister" ("תוֹחָאוּ" - "*wa-a-ho-wt*'"). The name "Naamah" means, "sweet, pleasant, delightful" and "beautiful," which seems to be at odds with the entire list of names in the seven generations of Cain. However, when one sees how "sweet iron" is a possible meaning, a different opinion can be reached about Tubal-cain's "sister."

"Sweet iron" is a name used to identify work hardened bits used to harness horses. While bridles are mostly leather strips linked by metal rings and fasteners, the bit, which goes into the horse's mouth, must be accepted by the horse. Harness and bridle makers have found that "sweet iron" has a taste that horses like, such that they accept the bridle; they can salivate on the iron. This plays a role in understanding the sister of a weapons craftsman.

Seeing sister Naamah as a tamer of horses, through the use of an iron bit that horses enjoy, means the metal weaponry that was the speciality of Tubal-cain could be used in tandem with his sister's specialty. Because horse riding equipment was her forte, with both siblings being metal workers the advancement that can be seen (if advancement is the right term to use) is the employment of horses in military pageantry, if not for use in battle.

When the information of this verse is seen in the light of mili-

Chapter 5: The lineage of Cain

tary advancement, the meaning of the next verse makes it easier to grasp that meaning. It must be realized that while Adam and Eve were in Heaven, they had tools that allowed them to sew fig leaves and scrape animal hides to make loincloths. These tools were rocks that were easily split to be sharp tools. As such, the crafting of metals into cutting blades goes beyond the need for skinning and food preparation. Because sweet iron bits are said to make a horse's mouth lather due to the bitterness of the rusting from the saliva, the same "sweetness" could be felt by Naamah, watching her harnesses be used in perverted religious rites. The same dulling of metal occurs when bronze or brass blades come into contact with bodily fluids, primarily blood.

This means the "invention" of metal instruments for war is the claim to fame of Zillah's twins to Lamech. This makes the use of "World-spear" be the purpose behind naming Tubal-cain. Since the family had begun moving around the land, spreading their religion as priests of lesser gods, they could use a show of strength while doing so. By having weapons in their possession that were unavailable to the common folk, with these having been made by the children of heroes, possessing uncommon strength, and with complete knowledge of what was good and what was evil, the advent of horsemen with spears would be a great advantage to the family of Cain.

It would begin the use of military force in exercising control over the hearts and minds of common human beings. It would begin the capture of slaves, harnessing them for the purpose of assisting their caravan movement. It could have meant the possibility for the occasional sacrifice of human life in a new blood rite. This awareness then plays into the meaning coming from the next verse.

Chapter 6

The eternal punishment of Cain

23 *And Lamech said unto his wives: Adah and Zillah, hear my voice; ye wives of Lamech, hearken unto my speech; for I have slain a man for wounding me, and a young man for bruising me;*

כג יִתְרְמָא הַנָּאָה, דְּמֵי יְשֵׁן--יְלוֹק וְעַמָּשׁ הַלָּצָן הַדַע, וִישָׁנָל דְּמֵי רְמָאיָנ: יִתְרְבֵּחַל דְּלֵן, יֶעְצְפַל יִתְגְרַה שִׁיא.

G3 *To say Lamech wife Adah Zillah to hear voice wife Lamech to listen speech for man to kill child to wound to strike.*

When the names in verse 23 are read as important meaning, one can read the whole verse as stating, "Said Humiliation (Lamech) to his wives that Ornament (Adah) and Darkness (Zillah), listen carefully. Outcries from women to Lowering (Lamech). Pay attention to this commandment for I have killed and wounded a child by striking." To understand this, one has to

Chapter 6: The eternal punishment of Cain

see Lamech (meaning Humiliation and Lowering) returning from a ritual performed with his sons and daughter assisting.

He meets his women, the mothers of his children, the two who ornament his life in darkness, and he tells them to listen carefully to the sounds that can be heard in the distance. Those sounds are the outcries of sorrow and pain from other mothers and wives who survived to mourn the sacrifices of slaves they knew and loved, from whom they had born children. They were offered to the gods of Lamech.

His ritual murders involved the use of sharp pointed metal blades on spears (lances), held against slaves bound in harnesses. They were captured through soldiers serving the temple, who held the advantage of having mighty metal-bladed weapons and attacked commoners by horseback. The women in the distance are crying loudly because their husbands and sons have been slain, "Lowered" to the ground. Perhaps they were interred, by "Lowering" into graves.

Lamech then issued a decree that all must realize (a speech or commandment), which announced he had killed a man, a human being, causing grief to ensue. The wives who were with child and the mothers with children too young to have been sacrificed survived with deep wounds that would never heal. The young boys would grow up to bear grudges (angers and resentments) that came from bearing witness to the strikes of battle and gods with no mercy. That would, in turn, cause them to seek revenge.

In other words, verse 23 is telling of the first swing of the pendulum of rage and hatred that is at the root of all war. It is why YAHWEH does not order the sacrifice of human beings, although the sacrifice of His Son, Jesus Christ, meant a heavenly reward. Lamech was repeating the act of his greatest forefather, Cain. The use of weapons previously unknown in battle would

The Cain & Abel Story

lead to a continuing cycle of forever furthering advancements in killing technologies.

Militaries would spread as a defensive need, until they had reached a level of strength that makes them an offensive strike to take land, rape women, and enslave people. The art of torture and blood sacrifice without fear of heavenly punishment had begun. No longer would bulls and lambs satisfy the gods of the "Lowered" world. Lamech, through the inventions of his sons and daughter, began a conquering mentality in lower minds that believed the gods favored one group of mankind over another and that it was okay to kill in the name of gods. Once that began, it could never be ceased.

---

24 *If Cain shall be avenged sevenfold, truly Lamech seventy and sevenfold.*

דכ יכ שְׁבַעֲתַיִם, יֻקַּם-קָיִן; וְלֶמֶךְ, שִׁבְעִים וְשִׁבְעָה.

D3 *When sevenfold to avenge Cain Lamech seventy seven.*

When one reads verse 23 as if Lamech realized what he thought was a good idea (human sacrifice) had turned out to be quite the opposite, here he recognized the Humiliation and Lowering that he must suffer. Because of his actions, which more than duplicated Cain's act of murder, Lamech recognized the sin of taking a human life cannot go unpunished. In front of his wives, Lamech decreed that he knows what his punishment will be.

It does not come from God speaking to him, as was the case

Chapter 6: The eternal punishment of Cain

with Cain, because Cain's descendants had turned away from YAHWEH. Lamech may have heard his voice of conscience speak to him, or he may have received some sign from Satan, but regardless of how he knew the consequence of his actions, he admitted it openly. Because Lamech appeared to know his punishment would be greater than Cain's, it may be that he welcomed a sentence that would forever place him under the control of evil.

By Lamech saying, "When sevenfold to avenge Cain," he is announcing that his children were that seventh and final generation of the initial sentence by Mother Earth. Nothing in Genesis 4 states that Cain had died, and none of the ages of Cain's children are listed to develop a time line. However, one may see how the Patriarchal timeline developed, up to the life of Noah, such that all before Noah had died by the time of the Great Flood.

The generations prior to the birth of Noah were nine (Noah the tenth). In that lineage, the descendant of Seth was named Lamech, and he was the ninth. That Lamech was the father of Noah. According to the Masoretic Text, Seth died not long before Noah was born, with Adam dying before Seth. According to the Syriac Pechitta Text, both Adam and Seth survive to see the birth of Noah. That lineage of heroes can indicate that Cain was still alive to witness the pronouncement of Lamech's punishment for his crime.

It can be assumed that Cain's punishment was to last seven generations. Had Cain influenced his generations of children to obey God and honor Him through their deeds, the sentence would have been served in full by the time his descendant Lamech sired the seventh generation. As Genesis 4 does a good job of projecting this was not the case, one can assume that when Cain did die he would not be allowed entrance into Heaven after

The Cain & Abel Story

death. Lamech proclaimed a further Lowering, as an extended Humiliation to Cain, as well as to all who would become the descendants of Lamech.

Seven generations of heroes could stretch anywhere to between 1,300 and 2,000 years. An additional seventy generations added would result in well over 10,000, if not 25,000 years. Following the Great Flood, the life span of human beings dropped, including those who share some DNA from Adam. Today, men live between 75 - 85 years. With a midpoint of that average life span (82.5 years), there would be 5,775 years added to the sentence of Lamech (70 X 82.5). A number like that becomes significant when the year 2014 is the Hebrew year 5775. In short, the meaning of Lamech's sentence appears to be intended to then bear the meaning, "Until the end of the world." In that case, the sentence will be automatically renewed because of the continuing evils unleashed by Lamech and his children.

In the field of study known as numerology, all numbered elements can be reduced to a one-digit number between one and nine. This relates to a base ten number system and does not recognize the value of zero. In addition to the one-digit reductions, there are what are called "master numbers," which have special significance.

Those master numbers are 11, 22, and 33. They are spiritual, more than physical, numbers with the numbers one, two, and three being multiplied by the number eleven. As such, for Lamech to say his punishment would be for seventy seven times in generations, the number 77 is the product of 7 times 11.

According to the website Whats-your-sign.com, a master number represents two of the same number. A repeated number must be understood, because two of the same number becomes twice as important. This means the number seven is important

Chapter 6: The eternal punishment of Cain

to understand as it applies to Cain, and doubly to Lamech. The website says this about the number "seven:"

> "Sevens, like Threes, deal with magical forces. Sevens deal with esoteric, scholarly aspects of magic. Representative of scholarly activities, mystery, and the focused search for esoteric meanings. Seven deals with the activation of imagination and manifesting results in our lives through the use of conscious thought and awareness. Ruled by Saturn, Seven can represent impractical dreaming, but with a deeper understanding of the aspects of Seven, you can quite deftly utilize its magical vibration to your own benefit."

This, simply through the repeated word "magic," can show the extended period of punishment that came from a deepening dependency on human intelligence. Our brains lock us to the earthly plane, rather than set a goal for the spiritual plane and God. From a "scholarly" approach to life, from which inventions manifest, the "activation of imagination" makes the earthly plane an illusion that keeps one distracted from God. We become trapped in the earthly plane because of our material minds. Adam and Eve fell from the grace of Heaven because their brains became activated by the fruit of knowledge.

This means "impractical dreaming" represents an attempt to secure one's "own benefit" over others. In this way, Lamech can be seen as celebrating his effect on humanity, as a servant to Satan. The sentence set upon the descendants of Cain, as the double number 77, was to master an ability to magically cast the world into a deep sleep, "Lowering" it further away from Heaven.

The Cain & Abel Story

With verse 24 the legacy of Cain is completed. Nothing more is said in the books of the Holy Bible about him or his descendants, directly. One can presume that all of the evils encountered by the main characters of the various books in the Holy Bible stem from the descendants of Cain, and the priests of Ba'al. By reading between the lines, the punishment stated by Lamech continued throughout the times of the Apostles and continues to this day.

Evil does not end this chapter in Genesis. As Cain was the only surviving son of Adam, at this point in the story, it makes sense that chapter 4 should end with a story of salvation. That is a repeating theme of the duality of the sin of Adam and Eve - knowing good and evil. A holy book demonstrates how evil always tries to deceive, but good can always overcome.

Cain begins a repeating pattern that will be found throughout the books of the Old Testament, one which Jesus would call the dead branches of the living vine and the wild grapes that must be kept away from the good grapes. Each dead branch changes from holy to unholy, just as Cain became a dead branch, no longer a point of biblical focus. As such, the gospel writer Luke presents the holy lineage of Jesus linking to Adam. That link goes through Seth, who had to be born because of Cain's sin, the murder of his younger twin.

Cain, as the eldest born son who fails his father and YAHWEH, begins a repeated theme in the Old Testament. In particular, the first born sons of Abraham (Ishmael), Isaac (Esau), and Jacob (Reuben – who defiled Jacob by begetting his half-brothers by sleeping with his mother's handmaid, with whom Jacob had slept) all failed their fathers and became dead branches, losing their rights to their father's blessing. The younger sons received the birthrights that ordinarily were designated for the

Chapter 6: The eternal punishment of Cain

first born son, each being blessed by their fathers (Isaac, Jacob, and Joseph). This theme means Adam would have to produce another son, who would replace Abel.

Chapter 7

The reincarnation of Abel

25 And Adam knew his wife again; and she bore a son, and called his name Seth: 'for God hath appointed me another seed instead of Abel; for Cain slew him.'

כה וַיֵּדַע אָדָם עוֹד, אֶת-אִשְׁתּוֹ, וַתֵּלֶד בֵּן, וַתִּקְרָא אֶת-שְׁמוֹ שֵׁת: כִּי שָׁת-לִי
אֱלֹהִים, זֶרַע אַחֵר--תַּחַת הֶבֶל, כִּי הֲרָגוֹ קָיִן.

H3 To know Adam again wife to beget son to call a name Seth for to put gods [Elohim] offspring another instead of Abel for to kill Cain.

Here the focus of Genesis 4 returns to Adam and Eve and the propagation of a lineage that will serve YAHWEH. Again, Adam becomes married to his wife through the penetration of his sperm into Eve's egg. The only function the sex act serves is to join husband and wife together physically, so God can marry them through a child. That creation is wholly in the hand of God.

Chapter 7: The reincarnation of Abel

Eve's comments reflect her knowledge of this spiritual influence.

The son that Eve gave birth to was named Seth. That represents the Hebrew word "*shath*" ("שֵׁת"), which means "foundation," and as "*shith*" ("שִׁת") "to put, set." For this reason, some say Seth means "Appointed." The same Hebrew letters produce a meaning of "buttocks, seat of the body," from the word "*shet*" ("שֵׁת"), and from that stems "*shethah*" ("הֹשָׁתָה"), meaning "drink." All play a role in defining the purpose of this name.

The reasoning for this name, as stated by Eve, is a replacement for Abel, who was killed by Cain. Therefore, the words written by Isaiah, translated as "sons of Seth," come from the Hebrew word "*she't*" or "*shachath*" ("תְּחַשׁ"), which means, "ruin" and "devastation." This means the name Seth fits one who is a "Foundation" of Abel, who has been "Put" on earth as the "Seat" of Abel, due to his "Ruin" at the hand of his brother Cain.

That meaning is an indication of the reincarnation of Abel, back into the "Seat of a body," which replaced the body lost. As such, when others see an alternate translation of "*shala*" or "*shethah*," meaning "drink," the fluidity implied by that word, and the implication of water, is then establishing a repeated theme of spirituality in the Holy Bible. This name tells us that Abel's soul is fluid and each life on earth is but one "Drink" of many.

When one embraces the concept of reincarnation as a standard element of our existence on earth, akin to our progressions through phases of life (such as the grades of schooling), it is nothing to fear. One's eyes are opened to an understanding of cycles and repetitions, of progressions and developments, regressions and failures. Reincarnation is a form of salvation, where the sins of the present life are forgiven at death, when a

The Cain & Abel Story

clean slate is the gift of God, as a new human life. Reincarnation means one is reborn with another chance to graduate to Heaven, as long as time does not end and one's soul has not been sold to Satan.

The element of Adam, the Son of God, is repeated in the element of Jesus, the Son of Man. The element of killing, which will become the Law of Moses as dictated by YAHWEH, has less impact as an act of evil, because no harm is ever done to a soul by death. The punishment given to Cain was not by YAHWEH, but by the Earth Goddess; and it was not for the sin of murder, but for the disrespect of spilling the blood of life on her soil.

One must realize that God (all-knowing) knew Cain would kill Abel. Because Abel killed a firstling in his offering to YAHWEH, killing a human being could be written off as not a sin. Sin can only be sin once known as such. YAHWEH let Cain know that, at which point Cain suggested he may kill again. For knowingly suggesting a repeat of his sin, the Father doled out extra punishment (sevenfold).

It is also vital to realize that the Hebrew text of verse 25 uses "*elohim*" and not YAHWEH ("*yhwh*" - "יְהוָה"). This plural form of "*El*," which means a singular "God," means our biological functions, which are extensions of YAHWEH, are themselves "gods." Genesis 2 says that on the seventh day all "gods" rested, and all "gods" blessed the creation the "gods" had made. In Genesis 2:4 we learn of the generations stemming from the man named Adam, by the LORD of all gods ("*YAHWEH elohim*" - "יְהוָה אֱלֹהִים").

We thus find, in Genesis 4:25, that it was the "gods" of "offspring" that "put" together the baby named Seth. This means all babies are produced by God, via God's microscopic helpers. It

Chapter 7: The reincarnation of Abel

also means that the souls themselves are "gods," simply because they are eternal, as the fingers of God operating on the material plane. Thus, the soul of Abel was a "god," which assisted the "gods" in the reproductive system of Eve, to create the life that would be Seth, filled with the eternal soul as Abel.

While we are all possessed by "gods," we can still be misled and tricked by other "gods," to do evil as did Cain. We have to be reminded of our dedication to God, through those "gods" within us, who always watch over us. This is the source of our guilt and conscience, and it is what leads us to find God. They are how we hear the voice of the LORD so we are urged to make the right decisions. Still, because there are good gods, on the earthly realm we have knowledge of evil gods too. Every step along the paths of our lives, we attract the influence of the earthly plane and the temptations to do evil.

A lesson like this one in Genesis 4 should act to make us focus on our role and responsibility for our salvation. We are advised to not let evil gain dominion over us. Regardless of all life's temptations, it is up to us to keep Satan from stealing our soul, by falling victim of an illusion that would cause one to sell a soul for nothing. We must learn the lesson that Cain teaches us, not to condemn ourselves to failure, where reincarnation means the karmic debt of sin has been left unpaid.

---

26 *And to Seth, to him also there was born a son; and he called his name Enosh; then began men to call upon the name of the LORD. {S}*

‏**וּ‎כ** תשֵׁלְוּ סג-אוּה דּלַיֵ-בְּ‎ו, אָרקָיוּ תאָ וּמשִׁ‎ נאֶוֹשׁ ;זאַ לחַוּה, אַרקָל שֵׁבָּ סמֶ
הוָהיְ. {ס}

The Cain & Abel Story

V3 *Seth also he beget son to call a name Enos at that time pierce to proclaim a name YHWH.*

This final verse of Genesis 4 tells what will come from the "Foundation" (Seth) of the first earthborn priest who would be dedicated to serving the needs of YAHWEH. Seth would begin to perfect a ministry for the LORD in a world that knew nothing of good and evil. The objective of this lineage is opposite that of the first-born son, Cain, whose separate lineage will forever attempt to lead human beings away from serving the One True God. Cain would begin a ministry that would teach human beings how to sin without remorse or knowing guilt. Seth would begin a line of priests who will bear the good fruit that will "Appoint" religion before the people, as examples of good, instead of wickedness.

The son born to Seth was named Enosh (or Enos), which means "Man Frail and Miserable" or "Mortal," "Human Being." One has to see how the wife of Seth, while unmentioned, was a female of creatures already established on the planet. Enosh's father, Seth, had come from two heroes, both of whom were made in Heaven, through the works of YAHWEH and the Earth Mother. The son named Cain was a "Shoot," empty of Spirit. The son named Seth, as a replacement for the "Vapor" of Abel, added a "Seat of body" for that "Spirit." Thus, Enosh would be born with the "Frailty" of an earthly mother, with "Human" traits sewn into the genetics of a hero priest. As such, Enosh would be the first to teach "Mortals" of a higher achievement being possible, through the exposure of the "Misery" an existence on earth becomes without the influence of religion.

All of the children begat by Cain were also the genetic blend-

Chapter 7: The reincarnation of Abel

ing of hero blood with earthly creatures. The difference was Cain sought to cover up his sin, through the Humiliation his punishment placed on him. Seth had no such reason to hide the teaching of moral restraint from Enosh, thus he would become the first "Human Being" seeking to make other human beings aware of One God and make sinful actions understood by all mankind.

Enosh being a priest is stated in the remainder of verse 26, which is translated as saying, "then began men to call upon the name of the LORD." This is the use of YAHWEH ("הוָֹהיְ"), which counters the use of *elohim* ("סיהִלֱאָ") in verse 25. The actual translation of the Hebrew says, "At that time to pierce" or "Then to bore," from "*ho-hal*" ("לחַוּה"), which leads one "to proclaim" ("*lik-ro*," from "אֹרְקִל"). This means the presence of Enosh "pierced" into those he encountered, causing a sensation that led the people "to call out" and "to scream."

This means an emotional connection was first established between God and ordinary "Human beings," through the priest Enosh. As such, the first hearts were pierced and the knowledge of good and evil, which opened eyes for that first awareness. For the first time mouths exclaimed guilt and praise to the One God, YAHWEH. No lesser gods would be able to comfort them from that point on.

Conclusion

The moral of the story

At the end of Genesis 4, we see that Adam and Eve had a replacement son for Abel. Genesis 5 then goes on to state, "This is the written account of Adam's family line." (Genesis 5:1a – NIV) It then begins, "When Adam had lived 130 years, he had a son in his own likeness, in his own image; and he named him Seth. After Seth was born, Adam lived 800 years and had other sons and daughters. Altogether, Adam lived a total of 930 years, and then he died." (Genesis 5:3-5 – NIV) That is a statement, through omission, that Cain and his descendants had been disowned.

The omission of Cain from Adam's branch of the living tree of God's children is taken to mean that never again would Adam's own flesh and blood have a place in Cain's life. This is important to grasp because it explains how Jesus could state, "If anyone comes to me and does not hate father and mother, wife and children, brothers and sisters--yes, even their own life--such a person cannot be my disciple." (Luke 14:26 – NIV)

Adam, the Son of God, and Jesus, the Son of Man (Adam),

Conclusion: The moral of the story

are truly dedicated to following the One God, YAHWEH, and no other god. Since all human beings are born of sin as earthly creatures, all mothers and fathers, wives, children, brothers, sisters, and yes, even one's self is filthy with earthly sin. Adam (and Eve) "hated Cain" for his sin, causing them to turn away from him and leave him to his chosen god. A true servant of YAHWEH would not turn away from Him, to go after one lost, such as Cain, who chose Lucifer.

In Luke we read of Jesus telling of the prodigal son, who also was the younger of two sons born to a father (one of the many places that parallel the Cain and Abel story). The son takes his share from his father's bounty (an advance on his inheritance) and leaves his home. The father lets him go, not following in sorrow, begging his son to come back, or trying to protect him from his waywardness. Only when the son returns on his own accord, with a personal realization of what he himself had lost, does the father welcome him back with open arms. This represents repentance, which Cain never showed.

In the story of the prodigal son we also see how there was a hint of animosity between the two sons,. The elder son became jealous of the special attention the father gave to younger, upon his having returned. The brother that never left never sinned, but the one who left did. Why would a sinner deserve special treatment?

That animosity was comforted by the father's explanation, "your brother was dead, and is alive; he was lost, and is found." (Luke 15:32b – NIV) The prodigal son had died, gone to Sheol, and was reborn into the robes of the Father. Salvation is always worth celebrating, while sin is left alone. God and Adam would have welcomed back Cain, had his story included likewise a soul-searching and epiphany, with him realizing that his own sins

The Cain & Abel Story

needed forgiveness. Only if Cain had returned to live as a servant to YAHWEH, reborn anew, would he cease to be as dead as Abel, lost in sin to Adam.

The lesson of the story of Cain and Abel is that we must not condone the sins of our children, our family members, or our neighbors and fellow Christians. We each must stay focused on God, with only prayers being sent to God that those lost may be found. There will be lost souls. Perhaps they will number many more than those who stay focused on God. But, with Christ's help we must remain true as living branches, producing good fruit.

The concept of *elohim* as multiple gods, and not a focus solely on YAHWEH, seems to be most difficult for Christians to grasp. God is the source of everything, and everything includes lesser gods. In that mix are both angels (good *elohim*) and demons (evil *elohim*); but we are not to be distracted by these many faces of God.

Still, to only see *elohim* as God is to only see the good of Creation. That narrow view blinds us from the influence of evil that stole Cain's soul. It has some question why God allows so much evil in the world.

In the Adam and Eve story, and into the Cain and Abel story, we see God talking directly to his human descendants. We also see a creature called a serpent speaking. As the stories get further from this source of origin, God does less direct communication with people, using more indirect methods as time moves on. In the physical realm, human kind is granted the grace of temporary incarnation, with free will to choose what course one will follow during a "worldly vacation." Cain followed the voice of sin, whereas Adam did not; the same options apply to us.

The fact that we believe God has angels means we believe

Conclusion: The moral of the story

in *elohim*. It does nothing to diminish YAHWEH by believing He has company, extensions of himself that are immortal and spiritual, not mortal and physical. When we believe that God created the Earth and God created Adam from the dust of earthly matter, it is then not disgracing God to believe God the Father mated with a goddess Mother. This makes all the creatures of Earth be God's children, through the union of God the Father with Mother Earth.

This union is in a most Spiritual way, but it is one most difficult to perceive. As such, the only way for us humans to comprehend it is through anthropomorphism. We imagine the gods (including YAHWEH) are in our image, so we can only imagine that they interact the same as we do. It is impossible for us to truly fathom how the unseen communicates, so we are told in ways that say, "Blood cries out to God from the ground."

This is how we have to read the plural number of *elohim* as a necessary multiplicity. When God created and said, "Let us make man in our image, in our likeness," (Genesis 1:26a) that states the plurality of two. We have the image of the physical joined with the image of the spiritual – Our Mother and Our Father.

The other lesson of Elohim is that there are many more spirits that rule over physical forms, which take great pleasure in influencing mankind to sin. Man is born into a world of sin, although the world itself is pure and natural, as long as it is not defiled by the lusts and greed that comes from human minds. We find the serpent as a natural creation of God, which was used as a test to sin. Cain fell under that influence and could not bring himself to redemption. He did not want to reject the lures of evil. Thus, Genesis 4 is about those who will fall from grace in the worldly realm.

The Cain & Abel Story

Adam was set up to fail, so Adam's sin would cause him to become God's gift to a world that needed knowledge of good and evil. Mankind needed a light to guide it away from the sins created by the *elohim* (gods) who had also fallen from grace. Satan (or Lucifer) led one-third of the immortal angels, those who refused to serve a mortal creature (Man), and as such the punishment given to those *elohim* was to have their immortal spirits trapped within the material realm.

The *elohim* of evil are powerless to force their will upon humans, but they are all-powerful in using their craftiness to entice humans to choose to sin. Sin turns a human's focus away from the spiritual and away from God. Thus, Adam would be the Son of God to influence man to serve YAHWEH, and not the evil *elohim* (gods).

Cain was the first-born son of Adam, who along with Abel, his younger twin, would be taught a life of dedicated service to YAHWEH. The story of Cain and Abel is important in that it shows one's pedigree is not the end-all to righteousness.

We see this repeated in the sons of Israel's most important prophets, who passed their torch to sons who would cheat the people, keeping the best parts of the sacrifice for themselves. We see this repeated in the Pharisees, Sadducees, and Temple priests, who used their positions to punish the faithful, while doing nothing to raise the faithful to self-sufficiency. We see this repeated today, every time some leader of a great Christian congregation is exposed as an addict to the power that being a great leader brings. It is the repeated theme of Cain lying down as a welcome mat at the doorway to evil, inviting sin to rule over him, doing nothing to stand up and tell Satan to serve him and YAHWEH.

The *elohim* are so prevalent today that we cannot turn around

Conclusion: The moral of the story

without putting our hands on another of countless things that have become our household idols. We lie down before the television. We lie down before the telephone. We lie down before the computer screen. We lie down before employers, politicians, religious leaders, friends and family members. We lie down for fancy cars, beautiful homes, and luxury vacations. We lie down before the *elohim* that trick us into taking a bite of the fruit from the tree of wealth, power, and influence, hearing the promise, "You can use it just like God and save the world."

We, therefore, cannot blame Cain because we are the reincarnation of Cain. We come from holy blood, but we have killed our chances of returning to be with the Father in Heaven. We are marked as sinners.

The good *elohim* stand by us, ready to lead us towards the right path; but the evil *elohim* stay in our ear, saying, "Just one more time, then you can quit." All *elohim* know the decision is ours to make, just as God told Cain, "If you do what is right, will you not be accepted? But if you do not do what is right, sin is crouching at your door; it desires to have you, but you must rule over it." (Genesis 4:7 – NIV) When we let our addictions rule us, we have become like Cain.

All one has to do is look at the downward spiral our Christian society (the West) has taken over the past 300 years, and especially over the last three generations. We have found religion becoming less important. We have found family becoming less important. We have found movement of populations away from the countryside and towards the cities.

When one sees how Cain built the first city and named it after his son, Enoch, we too have become wanderers. We move to and fro. We quiver in fear, praying more to our government to save us than to God. In cities, we have moved away from the bless-

The Cain & Abel Story

ings of Mother Earth and found a place where all the wayward and outcast are welcomed. We are welcomed there for no good reasons.

The purpose of Genesis 4 is to show how hard it is to pay the price of our own sins. From Cain's sevenfold punishment (seven generations of descendants) the digression led to a series of sins. One sin begetting more sins, ultimately to an exponential growth in punishments, all of which were self-imposed.

That is the miracle of the prodigal son's return home, after having squandered everything he had taken into his possession. The lost, dead son found happiness from being close to good, close to home. Even though he was mired in filth, he had positioned himself away from evil. He was content serving his time as an animal in the Father's care, rather than expecting to be a god owed everything. Many who become lost in sin follow a similar path as did Cain's family, led further and further into darkness, becoming too weak to swim against that tide.

The family of Cain paints a darker and darker image, one of sins compounding sins. To find the presence of horn and harps and metal works is not to find respite, but to find celebration of sin. It is representative of a state that revels in its state of debauchery.

It makes me think now of having gone to "churches" with bands playing, with guitar players and cymbal bashing drum players. They were playing alongside a horn section, with a choir wearing purple robes dancing to the music. The audience (not worthy of being called a congregation) was clapping and singing along, following the bouncing ball shown on the big screen monitor above the stage (not close to being an altar). That was the surrounding a truly fallen church, when the minister of ceremonies preached a message that said, "Jesus wants you to be

Conclusion: The moral of the story

rich!" That was the opposite of, "Walk into the light."

We must realize that Cain had the same hero blood as Adam, his father. Cain was placed on earth to be a priest. His failure did not send him out to slave the rest of his life as a farmer hoeing rock and hard earth for his survival. Cain took the easy way out, becoming a "professional priest," one who would sell religion as his job. Cain's family would progressively package worship services for a number of fallen *elohim*, each offering blessings for a price.

Cain became, in essence, the first "televangelist" or slicked down radio preacher pleading for funds, sounding like a goat with golden eyes and horizontal pupils bleating for recognition. His act was like going to a carnival and not being able to take your eyes off the mutants in the "freak show." He wanted people to lie down at the doorway of a circus show, one passing itself off as an influence for good, and promote that evil having dominion over them all.

The way to salvation, to become the prodigal son returning to the fold and again following YAHWEH with all your heart, is to see the importance of Seth being the reincarnation of Abel. When you sin and turn away from God it is hard to come back. You were Abel, pure and dedicated; but then Cain slew you. Thus you became Cain. To return to the LORD, you must slay Cain, being reborn as Seth. You must see Cain and Abel and Seth as you, all born of the Son of God, all to be reborn as the Son of Adam (the Son of Man).

In this scenario, Cain and Abel are not individual twins, but dual aspects of one's self. We each have the good side (Abel) within us. As youths we lean towards always doing good, wanting to help others, to honor our parents. But something always happens to make us become jealous of what others have, desiring

The Cain & Abel Story

the things we do not have. We let our countenance drop. Our own self-pity lowers our defenses to the point of letting ourselves rationalize evil as the right path to take. It is then that we rise up and strike our good self dead. We ask God, "What? Am I supposed to always maintain my positive side?"

In this view, our self-imposed punishment is to enter the labyrinth of life, where we enter into evil and temptation with only ourselves to save us. Every time we create some illusionary friend who pretends to help us survive our misery we are giving birth to another self-extension that is responsible for more self-imposed punishment. By the time we reach the level of Lamech, where we have encircled ourselves with enablers to the point of committing the most horrendous sins imaginable, we have lost this life and must endure many more reincarnations where the uphill climb is before us at each rebirth.

When we reach that dead end, we have become a dead branch. We are useless and are thrown into the fire. Our souls have been lost to Satan. That is why the promise of Seth is the promise of becoming the prodigal son. We can stand up and have dominion over evil. We can be reborn as the Son of Man and complete our intended purpose, to be a righteous priest to YAHWEH. In order to do that, we much receive the Holy Spirit.

In the Book of Luke, chapter 3, verse 38, we find the lineage of Jesus, as told by his mother Mary, to be linked to "the son of Enosh, the son of Seth, the son of Adam, the son of God." We must be linked to that same origin through Jesus. That does not mean we must be genetically related, but spiritually connected.

Just as Jesus was the Son of Man, we must be also. We must see the example of Jesus and become Jesus, by asking him to enter into our hearts. When Jesus hears our sincere plea for salvation, the Father sends the Holy Spirit in the name of Jesus

Conclusion: The moral of the story

Christ. Each of us who dedicates our lives to Christ, denouncing our sins, begging for forgiveness, can become Jesus. We must request to become another in the lineage of the Son of Man.

This is the Trinity, where we are the Son, connected to the Father by His love, the Holy Spirit. We intersect with all who have been the true priests of Adam, as all who shared the same Holy Spirit connection with YAHWEH. We must receive the spirit of desire for salvation, before we prove ourselves worthy of being the Son of Man.

Genesis 4 shows how hard it is to actually live up to our desires and prayers. Many are invited, but few are chosen. Many human beings have been born in the history of this world, but there have been only a few prophets of the LORD, those completely dedicated to His commands. Only one biblical Jesus has been born. Only one Ezekiel answering God's question, "Can these bones live," by responding, "You know." It is not a matter of wanting to have God chose you; it is up to you to choose.

Cain learned that God chose Abel's sacrifice, and not Cain's. The lesson of Genesis 4 is that we can go sit in a church and go through the motions of faith. We can put a few corn stalks, a couple of tomato plants, and a bag full of tubers into the offering plate, all things we took from the earth. We give nothing of our soul, because we only do as we are told, not as we feel. As a result, we never know the sheer joy of God looking at us; we become jealous of those who say, "The Holy Spirit is within me!" We pretend to be religious, while hiding our doubts.

We are not keeping our eyes to the Lord. Instead, we look around and see a friend who is sick. We see our bills not being paid. We see our offspring going down a path away from the church. We do not feel the Holy Spirit. We do not hear the LORD talking to us. We lower our countenance, and we fall

The Cain & Abel Story

away from God.

We pray for ourselves to be given what Abel received, without doing the work that is required. We never see Job as a model, where being tested by how many bad happening one can stand makes any reward received that much better. We do not want to find out how long we must slop the pigs, while longing for one pea pod of that slop being for ourselves, but not even getting that. We see how Cain reacted to not getting his way. The lesson of Genesis 4 is to see ourselves as more easily becoming a reproduction of Cain, and less inclined to be a willing sacrifice like Abel. The lesson of Genesis 4 is to become Seth.

In this book I have offered how my imaginations allow the evil of Cain's branch come to light. Due to my inabilities with Hebrew, I may be seeing much more than actually occurred. I may be giving Cain's lineage more credit for being evil than they deserve. You cannot dwell on the specifics of my guesses and hypotheses; but you can understand this line of Adam begat false religions that exist to this day, in all sizes, shapes and forms.

The purpose of this book is to expose Christians to the depth that comes from the Book of Genesis. There is much more than casually meets the eye. The tendency is to read the Holy Bible as a holy observer, seeing all the evil mentioned as the flaws to which others fall prey. It is time to start seeing each of us as the evil beings, such as Cain. We need to see that perspective.

I hope this conclusion has been helpful. I ask each reader to look at what I have seen and add more to that. The mind of God is so huge, you have something you can gain from it. Everything about the Holy Bible is meant to become a vehicle for a personal relationship with the Lord. See what you can find in Genesis 4, and every other chapter. They are all divinely inspired; and no Scripture is without deep meaning.

www.ingramcontent.com/pod-product-compliance
Lightning Source LLC
Chambersburg PA
CBHW020657300426
44112CB00007B/418